AN ESSENTIAL GUIDE TO BARBARA O'NEILL'S BOOK

WORKBOOK

SELF HEAL BY DESIGN

THE ROLE OF MICRO-ORGANISMS FOR HEALTH

JEN PRESS

For permissions contact: jenpress.workbooks@gmail.com
Workbook: Outlive: Self Heal By Design, First Edition
ISBN: 979-8860691285
Written by: Jen Press
Typesetting and text makeup by: Jen Press
Cover Image: Image by Freepik

Printed in the United States of America

This document is geared towards providing exact and reliable information in regards to the topic and issue covered. The publication is sold with the idea that the publisher is not required to render accounting, officially permitted, or otherwise, qualified services. If advice is necessary, legal or professional, a practiced individual in the profession should be ordered.

From a Declaration of Principles which was accepted and approved by a Committee of the American Bar Association and a Committee of Publishers and Associations.

MAKE THE CHANGE,
NOT ONLY FOR YOURSELF!

DONATION OPPORTUNITY

We believe that healing goes beyond the individual; it extends to the collective well-being of our communities and the world at large. As a token of our commitment to this belief, we are excited to offer you a unique opportunity to make a positive impact every time you engage with "Self Heal By Design" and this companion workbook.

Your Purchase Supports a Greater Cause

With every purchase of this accompanying workbook, a meaningful portion of the proceeds will be donated to charitable organizations dedicated to health, wellness, and environmental sustainability. Your choice to embark on this journey of self-healing doesn't just benefit you; it also contributes to causes that align with the book's message.

Thank you for being a part of this meaningful endeavor. Together, we can create a world where self-healing is not just a personal journey but a collective movement for positive change. Your contribution matters, and we are deeply grateful for your support.

YOUR FREE GIFT

As a way of saying thanks for your purchase, we are giving you best-selling workbooks for free.

Scan the QR-CODE below
and download the free workbooks immediately!

In addition to getting these workbooks for free, you'll also have an opportunity to get our newest books for free, enter giveaways, and receive other valuable emails from us.

If you have any questions, suggestions for us
or want to work with us, shoot us an email at:

jenpress.workbooks@gmail.com

NOTE

We would like to inform you that this summary and analysis workbook of "Self Heal By Design- The Role Of Micro-Organisms For Health By Barbara O'Neill" is a plagiarism-free resource created to complement your original reading experience, not to substitute it.

Our intention in producing this summary and analysis workbook is to provide you with a helpful tool that can enrich your understanding and engagement with the original book. It is not intended to replace the original source material, which we highly recommend you purchase and read in its entirety.

We strongly encourage you to purchase the original book, by scanning the QR code below, you will be directed directly the Amazon:

TABLE
OF CONTENTS

WORKBOOK OVERVIEW

In the introduction section of this workbook, we will provide you with an overview of the book "Self Heal By Design" and how to effectively use this workbook as a companion to the main text. We will explain the purpose of the book and how it can be a valuable resource for your personal journey of self-healing.

We will start by setting the stage for your personal journey of self-healing. This section will encourage you to reflect on your own health and wellness goals and how the concepts presented in the book can be applied to your life. It will help you establish a connection between the book's content and your own experiences.

Sickness Is No Accident: The body has a plan. In this chapter, we will explore the idea that the human body has an innate plan for health and healing. We will delve into the concept that illness is not a random occurrence but often a result of imbalances in the body's natural processes.

Historical Moments: What does the past tell us?. Here, we will delve into historical events and discoveries that have shaped our understanding of health and disease. We will examine how the lessons from the past can inform our present approach to wellness.

Familiarizing With A Fungus Feast. This chapter will focus on the intriguing concept of a "fungus feast" and its implications for health. We will explore the role of fungi in our environment and its potential impact on our well-being.

Mycology The Study of Fungi. A deeper understanding of the science of mycology, the study of fungi, will be provided in this section. We will examine the significance of mycology in the context of health and its potential to shed light on various health issues.

Presenting the Evidence, History of Fungus: The role fungus plays in Human Disease. This chapter will present historical evidence linking fungus to human diseases. We will explore case studies and research findings that highlight the role of fungi in various health conditions.

The Link Between Fungus And Cancer. The connection between fungal infections and cancer will be discussed in detail in this chapter. We will explore the research and theories surrounding this link and its implications for cancer prevention and treatment.

The Role of Genes in Disease: Are we in bondage to defective Genes?. We will delve into the role of genetics in the development of diseases and whether our genetic makeup binds us to certain health conditions. This chapter will encourage you to question common assumptions about genetics and disease.

Fuel for Life: Food performs or deforms. Your diet plays a crucial role in your health. This chapter will emphasize the impact of your food choices on your overall well-being and provide guidance on making informed dietary decisions.

Conquering Candida And Other Fungus/Yeast Related Problems. Strategies for addressing and overcoming issues related to candida and other fungal infections will be explored in this chapter. Practical tips and solutions will be provided.

Acid and Alkaline Balance: Precision is everything. Maintaining a balanced pH level in the body is essential for health. This chapter will dive into the significance of acid and alkaline balance and how it affects various bodily functions.

The Stomach's Secret Weapon: Hydrochloric acid and digestion. The role of hydrochloric acid in the digestive process will be thoroughly examined in this chapter. You will gain insight into how this "secret weapon" in your stomach contributes to your overall well-being.

Liver: The project manager. The final chapter will shed light on the liver's crucial role as the "project manager" of your body's functions. Understanding the liver's functions is essential for optimizing your health.

This workbook has been designed to complement your reading of "Self Heal By Design." It includes exercises, reflection questions, and activities tailored to each chapter's content, aiming to empower you to apply the book's concepts to your own life and embark on a journey of self-healing and improved well-being.

INTRODUCTION

OVERVIEW OF "SELF HEAL BY DESIGN"

"RETHINKING MEDICINE TO LIVE BETTER LONGER"

"Self Heal By Design: The Role of Micro-Organisms for Health" by Barbara O'Neill opens the door to a realm of health and vitality that few of us fully comprehend. In an era where scientific discoveries are reshaping our understanding of the human body, O'Neill takes us on a captivating journey into the microscopic world within us—our microbiomes. These communities of microorganisms, including bacteria, viruses, fungi, and other tiny life forms, are not merely passengers within our bodies; they are active participants in our health and well-being.

Barbara O'Neill, a renowned expert in natural health and nutrition, brings her wealth of knowledge to this compelling book. With meticulous research and clear, accessible writing, she unveils the intricate interplay between these micro-organisms and the intricate systems that make up the human body. Through "Self Heal By Design," O'Neill empowers readers to harness the potential of these microscopic allies to achieve optimal health.

The core premise of the book revolves around the concept that our microbiomes are not merely an accessory to our health but are, in fact, the architects of our well-being. They play a crucial role in digestion, immunity, metabolism, and even our mental health. The balance and diversity of these microorganisms can determine whether we thrive or struggle with health issues.

Drawing from the latest scientific research, O'Neill dissects the fascinating relationship between our microbiomes and various health conditions. From digestive disorders to autoimmune diseases, from obesity to mental health concerns, she unravels the intricate web of connections that link the health of our microbiomes to our overall physical and mental wellness. This book serves as a vital guide for anyone seeking to better understand their body and explore natural, holistic ways to enhance their health.

What sets "Self Heal By Design" apart is its practical approach to microbiome optimization. O'Neill not only educates readers on the importance of these micro-organisms but also provides actionable strategies to nurture and support them. Through dietary recommendations, lifestyle adjustments, and natural remedies, readers will learn how to create an environment within their bodies that fosters a thriving and diverse microbial ecosystem.

In an age where antibiotic overuse, processed foods, and environmental toxins have taken a toll on our microbiomes, "Self Heal By Design" offers a beacon of hope. It presents an opportunity for individuals to take charge of their health by making informed choices that positively impact their microbial communities. The book equips readers with the knowledge and tools necessary to embark on a transformative journey towards greater vitality and resilience.

In conclusion, "Self Heal By Design: The Role of Micro-Organisms for Health" by Barbara O'Neill is a must-read for anyone seeking a holistic and scientifically-backed approach to health and wellness. Through the pages of this book, readers will gain a profound understanding of the pivotal role that microorganisms play in our lives. They will also discover the keys to unlocking their full potential for self-healing and well-being. Join us as we embark on this enlightening voyage into the hidden world within, and embark on a path towards a healthier, more vibrant you.

ABOUT THE AUTHOR

Barbara O'Neill is a highly regarded figure in the field of natural health and nutrition. Her journey into this realm began with a personal quest for better health, leading her to explore various natural healing modalities. Over the years, she has earned diplomas in Naturopathy and Nutritional Medicine, continually expanding her knowledge.

What sets Barbara O'Neill apart is her ability to simplify complex scientific information, making it accessible and practical for everyday people. She is a sought-after speaker and educator, conducting seminars and workshops worldwide.

Her latest book, "Self Heal By Design: The Role of Micro-Organisms for Health," reflects her passion for empowering readers to understand and optimize their microbiomes for better health. Barbara O'Neill's work continues to inspire and transform lives, offering a holistic approach to well-being rooted in scientific understanding and a deep respect for the body's natural healing abilities.

HOW TO USE IT

Welcome to the workbook companion for "Self Heal By Design: The Role of Micro-Organisms for Health" by Barbara O'Neill. This workbook is designed to enhance your reading experience and help you apply the valuable insights and practical advice from the book to your own life. Here's how to make the most of this resource:

1. Read the Book First: Before diving into this workbook, it's essential to read the main book, "Self Heal By Design," by Barbara O'Neill. The workbook is meant to complement the information presented in the book, so you'll benefit most if you have a solid understanding of the concepts discussed in the main text.

2. Set Clear Goals: Begin by defining your goals for using this workbook. What specific aspects of your health and well-being are you looking to improve or understand better? Are you interested in optimizing your microbiome, managing a specific health condition, or simply adopting a healthier lifestyle? Knowing your goals will help you focus your efforts.

3. Chapter Alignment: Each section of this workbook corresponds to a chapter in the main book. To get started, match the workbook section to the relevant chapter you've read. This alignment will help you apply the concepts discussed in the book directly to your life.

4. Reflect and Record: In each workbook section, you'll find questions, prompts, and exercises designed to encourage reflection and self-assessment. Take the time to journal your thoughts and answers. This process will help you internalize the information and apply it to your unique circumstances.

5. Set Actionable Steps: After reflecting on the concepts from the book, identify actionable steps you can take to improve your health and well-being. These might include dietary changes, lifestyle adjustments, or specific practices recommended by Barbara O'Neill. Be specific about what you plan to do and when you will implement these changes.

6. Track Your Progress: Use the space provided in this workbook to track your progress. Note any improvements in your health, energy levels, or overall well-being as you implement the recommendations from the book. Tracking your progress will help you stay motivated and adjust your approach as needed.

7. Seek Support and Guidance: If you encounter challenges or have questions along the way, don't hesitate to seek support and guidance. Whether it's consulting a healthcare professional, joining online forums, or reaching out to Barbara O'Neill's community, there are resources available to assist you on your journey to better health.

8. Stay Committed: Remember that lasting change takes time and commitment. Stay patient and persistent as you work toward your health goals. Regularly revisit this workbook to assess your progress and make necessary adjustments.

By following these steps and using this workbook as a tool for self-discovery and improvement, you'll be well on your way to harnessing the power of your microbiome and optimizing your health according to the principles outlined in "Self Heal By Design." Here's to your journey towards a healthier, more vibrant you!

YOUR JOURNEY

These blank pages have been intentionally left empty to provide you with a space where you can reflect on your journey as you read through the book. Use this space to write down your goals, intentions, and aspirations for this journey. You can also take some time to reflect on your past experiences and how they have impacted your life.

By jotting down your thoughts and feelings, you will be able to compare your growth and progress at the end of this book. This workbook is designed to help you gain a deeper understanding of yourself and how to use fasting to your advantage. Take advantage of this opportunity to create a roadmap for your healing journey.

Remember, this is your personal journey, and there is no right or wrong way to go about it. Allow yourself to be vulnerable, and embrace the process with an open mind. We hope that this workbook serves as a helpful tool in your healing journey.

CHAPTER 1:
SICKNESS IS NO ACCIDENT
THE BODY HAS A PLAN

Summary

"It is highly dishonourable for a reasonable soul, living in so divinely a built mansion as the body she resides in, to be totally unacquainted with its exquisite structure."
— Robert Boyle, 1690

This chapter emphasizes the importance of understanding and taking care of the human body. The author states that the human body is a self-healing organism, but many people suffer from sickness due to a lack of knowledge about the conditions necessary for healing. The book aims to explore the reasons behind this issue that even massive medical expenditure has failed to solve.

The author draws a comparison between how people understand and maintain complex machinery like cars, airplanes, and computers, and how little they know about their own bodies. The chapter highlights the lack of knowledge about the working and care required to keep the human body in optimal condition for a smooth and trouble-free life journey.

The discussion then shifts to the cycle of life, which applies to all living things. This cycle of life and death also has a profound impact on human health, and the author expresses a desire to explore the connections between this cycle and sickness in the human body.

The chapter ends with a reference to Rudyard Kipling's poem, suggesting its relevance to the concept being discussed.

"I have six trusty serving men, They taught me all I know, Their names are What, Why, When, Where, How, and Who."

DUST TO DUST: THE CYCLE OF LIFE

The passage discusses the concept of the Carbon Cycle and the role of microorganisms in nature, particularly focusing on fungi. The Carbon Cycle refers to the process by which living matter is broken down and returned to dust upon death.

Microorganisms, such as bacteria, fungi, and yeast, play a crucial role in this cycle, breaking down dead matter and returning essential nutrients and minerals to the soil for nourishing plants and other organisms. The text explains that microorganisms are responsible for the decomposition of organic matter, effectively recycling it and ensuring that nutrients are made available for new life forms.

The passage provides a practical example of the Carbon Cycle in action through compost bins. Three bins are described: the first bin receives kitchen food scraps and garden weeds mixed with cow manure. The second bin allows the carbon cycle to work and decompose the organic matter. The third bin contains the end product - the decomposed vegetable matter turned to dust, which can now be used to enrich the garden soil. This decomposition process is made possible by the activities of microorganisms present in the compost.

MICROORGANISMS IN THE DUST

The focus then shifts to microorganisms in the soil. Bacteria, fungi, and yeast form a significant part of the microscopic life in the soil. They play a vital role in breaking down dead matter and releasing essential nutrients and minerals like calcium, phosphate, and potassium back into the soil, where they can nourish plants and other organisms. The fungi are particularly noteworthy as they can thrive even in harsh environments, including rocks and mineral-rich soil. They can remain inactive or dormant for extended periods until a suitable food source becomes available.

The passage delves into the characteristics of fungi and their importance in nature. Fungi are eukaryotic organisms that lack chlorophyll and cannot perform photosynthesis like plants. They reproduce by spore formation and obtain nutrition from their surroundings, which may include dead or non-living organic substances. Some fungi can act as parasites, feeding off living organisms, including humans, while others function as saprophytes, consuming dead organisms and acting as nature's garbage collectors.

The author highlights the importance of fungi in the ecosystem as they break down dead matter and participate in the carbon cycle. They also play a role in producing carbon dioxide in the soil for plant respiration and aid in converting metals and minerals into absorbable forms for plants.

MICROORGANISMS IN PLANTS

Next, the passage explores the role of microorganisms in plants. The plant secretes glucose into its roots, which benefits surrounding microorganisms. These microbes assist the plant in various ways, such as fixing nitrogen from the atmosphere, recycling minerals from plant residues, removing toxins, stabilizing locked-up phosphorus, producing growth stimulants, and protecting the plant from pathogens.

The same microorganisms that aid in the growth and development of plants also contribute to their breakdown. As an example, the passage explains how microorganisms are involved in the development, ripening, and eventual decomposition of an apple. The role, phase, function, and form of each microorganism are dictated by the environment.

The passage further examines the classification of fungi, which has been a concern since the 17th century because fungi exhibit characteristics of both animals and plants. Despite lacking chlorophyll and not performing photosynthesis, fungi are essential as they act as nature's clean-up team by breaking down dead matter and returning it to dust as part of the Carbon Cycle.

MICROORGANISMS IN THE EGG

Moving on, the text discusses microorganisms in eggs. The development of an egg into a chicken is attributed to the microorganisms present in the white and yolk of the egg. Even a damaged egg can be a part of the Carbon Cycle, as the cell damage caused by shaking results in microorganisms transforming into bacteria, yeast, fungus, and mold to break down the damaged tissue.

MICROORGANISMS IN HUMANS

The focus then shifts to microorganisms in humans. Surprisingly, the human body contains more microorganisms than cells, leading the author to question whether humans are more plant-like than animal-like. The largest concentration of microorganisms in the human body is found in the gastrointestinal tract, where they play a role similar to that in the soil, breaking down nutrients for absorption, specifically the B vitamins.

Beneficial bacteria such as Acidophilus and Bifidus live permanently in the gastrointestinal tract and aid in nutrient absorption while protecting against harmful microbes. However, there are many other transient bacteria, yeast, and fungi that can live on the skin, hair, in the mouth, intestines, and on the food consumed. Candida albicans, a yeast, plays a crucial role in the chemical balance of the intestines, and Acidophilus and Bifidus bacteria prevent its overgrowth.

The passage highlights that understanding the role of microorganisms in nature provides insights into how they can affect humans. Beneficial microorganisms help in nutrient absorption and protection, while harmful fungi, which feed off living organisms, can cause diseases in humans. Some of the diseases caused by pathogenic fungi include athlete's foot, swimmer's ear, ringworm, dandruff, fingernail and toenail infections, rosacea, and yeast infections.

The passage concludes with a note on the growth of fungi, explaining that they sprout from spores and grow filaments called hyphae, enabling them to penetrate various surfaces, including plant cell walls, human skin, and nails. Yeast can grow at body temperature, making athlete's foot a systemic condition that can penetrate deep into tissues.

In summary, the passage extensively explores the Carbon Cycle and the essential role of microorganisms, especially fungi, in breaking down dead matter and returning it to dust. The presence of microorganisms in soil, plants, eggs, and the human body illustrates their significance in natural processes and ecosystem functioning. Understanding their roles provides insights into how they can impact nature, plants, animals, and humans, both positively and negatively.

A LIVING ILLUSTRATION

The passage describes the Carbon Cycle in the context of human health, focusing on Sick Steve, a heavy smoker, and his brother Healthy Harry. Steve's constant cell damage in his lungs from smoking leads to his body's microorganisms attempting to repair the damage. When their cousin, Colin, with a bad cold coughs on both Steve and Harry, the bacteria from Colin enter their bodies. While Steve becomes sick, Harry remains unaffected due to his healthier lifestyle and diet.

Steve seeks medical help and is prescribed antibiotics, which alleviate his cold symptoms but also kill off beneficial bacteria in his lungs and gut. This leads to an overgrowth of Candida albicans yeast in his intestines, causing various health issues. The passage highlights how antibiotics can disrupt the balance of microorganisms in the body.

Steve's overgrowth of yeast causes fungal outbreaks, and he returns to the doctor for treatment. However, the antifungal medication, nystatin, exacerbates the problem by allowing the fungus to mutate and penetrate deeper into his tissues.

Overall, the author emphasizes the importance of lifestyle and diet choices in maintaining health and the potential consequences of disrupting the body's natural microorganism balance. It suggests that Steve's ignorance about the impact of his habits is contributing to his declining health.

CAUSE AND EFFECT

Newton's third law of motion states that: "To every action there is an equal and opposite reaction" or, simply put, the law of cause and effect. "This law never ceases to act as the perfect balancer. Nature's equalizer; set- ting into motion compensatory forces to remedy every imbalance," says David Phillips in his book From Soil to Psyche.

ANTIBIOTICS—ARE THEY FRIEND OR FOE?

This part discusses antibiotics, their origins, impact on the body, and long-term effects. In 1928, Alexander Fleming discovered penicillium, a mould that produced a mycotoxin called penicillic acid, which is more toxic than the mould itself. This mycotoxin is designed to kill off competing organisms to ensure the mould's survival.

Antibiotics have saved millions of lives by eliminating harmful bacteria and their toxic waste. However, the overuse of antibiotics and the lack of questioning the active presence of bacteria, yeast, and fungus in the body pose dangerous consequences. Some doctors claim that antibiotics are causing more problems than they solve.

The discovery of penicillium led to testing hundreds of mycotoxins as possible antibiotics, but 80 percent of them were too toxic to use. Antibiotics are both antibacterial and antihuman substances, killing not only harmful bacteria but also healthy bacteria in the gut, such as bifidus bacterium and lactobacillus acidophilus. This disruption allows yeast like Candida albicans in the gut to multiply rapidly.

The passage also mentions yeast's rapid multiplication, evident in yeast bread doubling in half an hour.

In summary, antibiotics have played a crucial role in saving lives by eliminating harmful bacteria. However, their overuse can lead to adverse effects by disrupting the balance of microorganisms in the body, including beneficial bacteria, and promoting the rapid growth of opportunistic pathogens like Candida albicans. It emphasizes the need for responsible antibiotic use and understanding their potential consequences on the body.

LESSONS AND KEY POINTS FROM THIS CHAPTER

1. Importance of Understanding and Caring for the Human Body: The chapter stresses the significance of understanding and taking care of the human body to promote self-healing and overall well-being. Lack of knowledge about healing conditions can lead to sickness and health issues.

2. Comparison to Complex Machinery: The chapter draws a comparison between people's understanding of complex machinery and their lack of knowledge about their own bodies. It highlights the need for better education and awareness about body maintenance.

3. The Cycle of Life: The chapter explores the universal cycle of life and death and its impact on human health. Understanding this cycle can provide insights into sickness and the body's healing processes.

4. Microorganisms in Nature: The passage discusses the role of microorganisms, particularly fungi, in the Carbon Cycle. Microorganisms are crucial for decomposing organic matter and recycling nutrients, benefiting the ecosystem.

5. Microorganisms in Humans: The passage explains the significant presence of microorganisms in the human body, especially in the gastrointestinal tract. Beneficial bacteria aid in nutrient absorption, while harmful fungi can cause diseases if they overgrow.

6. Consequences of Antibiotics: The section on antibiotics highlights their life-saving potential but also warns against overuse. Antibiotics can disrupt the body's natural microorganism balance, leading to health issues like Candida albicans overgrowth.

7. Impact of Lifestyle and Diet: The living illustration of Sick Steve and Healthy Harry demonstrates the influence of lifestyle and diet choices on health. A healthier lifestyle can better equip the body to fight off infections and maintain balance.

8. Cause and Effect: The mention of Newton's third law emphasizes the law of cause and effect, which applies to both natural and human systems. Understanding the consequences of actions is essential in maintaining health and balance.

REFLECTION QUESTIONS

These questions can help guide your reflection on the chapter and facilitate a deeper understanding of the author's message and ideas.

How do you currently prioritize your understanding of your own body and its self-healing abilities in comparison to other aspects of your life?

Reflect on your knowledge about the Carbon Cycle and the role of microorganisms in nature. How can you apply this understanding to make informed decisions about your health and well-being?

What lifestyle choices or habits do you think might be negatively impacting your health and disrupting the balance of microorganisms in your body?

Consider the story of Sick Steve and Healthy Harry. How does this story resonate with your own health choices and lifestyle? Are there areas where you can make positive changes?

How do you approach the use of antibiotics in your own life? Are you aware of their potential long-term effects on your body's microorganism balance?

Reflect on the concept of cause and effect in the context of your health decisions. What actions can you take to create a balanced and healthier lifestyle that promotes well-being?

MILESTONE GOALS

Develop a deeper understanding of the Carbon Cycle and the role of microorganisms in nature to gain insights into the interconnectedness of life processes and how they impact human health.

Reflect on personal lifestyle choices and habits that might be detrimental to health, and work towards making informed decisions to promote a balanced and healthier lifestyle that supports the body's self-healing abilities.

Increase awareness about the responsible use of antibiotics and their potential long-term effects on the body's microorganism balance, leading to a more cautious approach towards antibiotic usage and exploring alternative ways to support the immune system and overall well-being.

ACTIONABLE MOVEMENTS

1. Embrace a plant-based diet:

- Include a variety of fresh fruits, vegetables, whole grains, legumes, nuts, and seeds in your daily meals.
- Set a goal to try at least two new plant-based recipes each week.
- Reduce or eliminate processed and sugary foods from your diet.

2. Foster a healthy gut microbiome:

- Consume foods rich in probiotics, such as yogurt, kefir, sauerkraut, or kimchi, to support gut health.
- Add prebiotic foods like garlic, onions, and bananas to your meals, which feed beneficial gut bacteria.
- Avoid unnecessary antibiotic use and discuss with your healthcare provider if antibiotics are genuinely necessary.

3. Practice mindful eating:

- Take time to eat without distractions and savor each bite, paying attention to hunger and fullness cues.
- Avoid overeating by stopping when you feel satisfied rather than stuffed.
- Listen to your body and choose foods that nourish and energize you.

4. Engage in regular physical activity:

- Commit to at least 30 minutes of moderate exercise, such as brisk walking or cycling, on most days of the week.
- Explore different types of physical activities to find what you enjoy.
- Incorporate movement breaks throughout the day, even if it's just stretching or taking short walks.

5. Reduce exposure to harmful substances:

- Limit or quit smoking and avoid exposure to secondhand smoke.
- Minimize the use of toxic household cleaners and opt for natural alternatives.
- Choose organic produce whenever possible to reduce exposure to pesticides.

6. Foster a positive mindset:

- Practice gratitude by writing down three things you are grateful for each day.
- Engage in activities that bring joy and reduce stress, such as spending time in nature, reading, or pursuing hobbies.
- Surround yourself with supportive and positive individuals who uplift your well-being.

7. Educate yourself and others:

- Read books and articles on health, nutrition, and the human body to deepen your knowledge.
- Share your learnings with friends and family, promoting awareness of the importance of taking care of the body and its self-healing capabilities.
- Encourage open discussions about responsible antibiotic use and its potential consequences on overall health.

Remember that implementing these actionable movements may require gradual changes and persistence. Set realistic goals and celebrate your progress along the way. Stay committed to improving your health and well-being, making conscious choices that align with the understanding gained from this chapter.

Record your reflections, insights, and observations on the concepts discussed earlier.

Use this space to brainstorm, sketch, or jot down any questions that arise in your mind. Make it a truly personal experience.

CHAPTER 2:
HISTORICAL MOMENTS
WHAT DOES THE PAST TELL US?

Summary

The chapter delves into the historical and evolving understanding of the role of fungus in human diseases over the last two centuries. It highlights significant thinkers who have contributed to this theory and provides an illustrative example from history to support the idea.

One notable figure discussed is Florence Nightingale (1820–1910), renowned for her pioneering work as a nurse during the Crimean War. In the midst of deplorable conditions at a military hospital, she managed to drastically reduce the death rate through improved hygiene, sanitation, and nutrition. Her insights are encapsulated in her book "Notes on Nursing" (1860), where she suggests that disease, often seen as harmful, could be interpreted as a reparative process by the body. She posits that disease is an effort of nature to counteract processes of poisoning or decay that might have occurred long before the noticeable symptoms appear.

Florence Nightingale's perspective shifts the perspective of disease, viewing it as a means of repairing the body, provided the right conditions are established. Her assertion is that hindering this natural repair process, through factors like drugs, malnutrition, or lack of proper healthcare, could lead to dire consequences, even death. Moreover, she underscores the role of microorganisms, particularly fungi, in aiding the body's healing efforts.

Another luminary mentioned is Professor Antoine Bechamp (1816-1908), a French scientist known for his extensive research on microscopic life forms. His experiments, including sealing a dead cat in an airtight container, demonstrated the transformation of microorganisms within the cat's remains. Bacteria, yeast, and mold successively played roles in breaking down the cat's body, ultimately reducing it to dust. Bechamp's observations reinforce the idea of microorganisms, including fungi, participating in natural cycles of life and decomposition.

In summary, the chapter explores the historical context of the theory that fungus plays a significant role in human diseases. It highlights Florence Nightingale's groundbreaking perspective on disease as a reparative process and Antoine Bechamp's experiments that provide tangible evidence of microorganisms' involvement in the natural cycle of life and decay. This theory challenges conventional notions of disease and underscores the potential interplay between microorganisms, particularly fungi, and human health. By revisiting the insights of these historical figures, we gain a deeper understanding of the complex relationship between the human body and microbial life.

LESSONS AND KEY POINTS FROM THIS CHAPTER

1. **Alternative Perspective on Disease:** The chapter introduces an alternative perspective on disease, challenging the conventional notion that disease is solely harmful. It suggests that disease might actually be a reparative process by which the body attempts to counteract earlier processes of poisoning or decay.

2. **Microorganisms and Healing:** The chapter emphasizes the role of microorganisms, particularly fungi, in both the breakdown of organic matter and the healing process. These microorganisms are depicted as essential players in the cycle of life and decomposition.

3. **Hygiene and Health:** Florence Nightingale's work during the Crimean War serves as a powerful lesson in the importance of hygiene, sanitation, and proper nutrition in maintaining health and reducing disease. Her efforts led to a significant reduction in the death rate at a military hospital.

4. **Natural Repair and Hindrance:** The idea that the body's natural repair processes can be hindered by factors such as drugs, malnutrition, and neglect of health principles highlights the delicate balance required for maintaining well-being.

5. **Microscopic Life Forms:** Antoine Bechamp's experiments with microorganisms, where he observed their roles in decomposition and transformation, underscore the complex interactions between these tiny life forms and their impact on larger biological processes.

6. Florence Nightingale's innovative approach to nursing during the Crimean War resulted in substantial reductions in the death rate at a military hospital through improved hygiene and nutrition.

7. Nightingale's "Notes on Nursing" presents the idea that disease might be a natural reparative process aimed at countering earlier poisoning or decay in the body.

8. The disease can be seen as a way for the body to repair itself, but this process can be hindered by factors like drugs, malnutrition, and neglect of health principles.

9. Microorganisms, including bacteria, yeast, and mold, play vital roles in the natural cycle of life and decomposition, as demonstrated by Antoine Bechamp's experiments.

10. Fungi, in particular, are highlighted as significant participants in the process of breaking down organic matter, underlining their potential role in both disease and healing.

11. Bechamp's research suggests that microorganisms evolve and transform in response to changing environmental conditions, contributing to the dynamic nature of biological systems.

12. The chapter encourages readers to reconsider their understanding of disease and microbial life, challenging the conventional view and highlighting the intricate relationship between human health and the natural world.

REFLECTION QUESTIONS

How does the notion of disease as a reparative process reshape your understanding of health and influence your attitude towards illness and medical interventions?

In what ways can you incorporate Florence Nightingale's emphasis on hygiene and sanitation into your daily routine to enhance your overall well-being?

Reflecting on the role of microorganisms in natural processes, how might you strike a balance between maintaining a clean environment and fostering a healthy microbial ecosystem?

Considering the potential hindrance of the body's natural repair processes by factors like drugs and malnutrition, how can you ensure that your lifestyle choices support and optimize your body's healing mechanisms?

How open are you to challenging conventional beliefs about health and exploring alternative perspectives? How might adopting a more open mindset impact your approach to personal health and wellness decisions?

MILESTONE GOALS

Broaden Understanding of Disease and Health: Your first goal could be to expand your comprehension of disease and health by embracing the alternative perspective presented in the chapter. Strive to grasp the concept of disease as a potential reparative process and explore how this outlook might alter your perception of health challenges and the body's natural healing mechanisms.

Integrate Hygiene and Lifestyle Practices: Inspired by Florence Nightingale's emphasis on hygiene and sanitation, your second goal could be to incorporate these practices into your daily routine. Aim to enhance your well-being by adopting better hygiene habits and maintaining a cleaner environment, recognizing the potential impact these practices can have on disease prevention and overall health.

Promote Open-Mindedness and Critical Thinking: Your third goal could be to cultivate a greater sense of open-mindedness and critical thinking when it comes to health-related concepts. Strive to challenge established beliefs, explore alternative theories, and question conventional approaches to health and wellness. By nurturing a mindset of curiosity and exploration, you can better navigate the complexities of health and make informed decisions for your well-being.

ACTIONABLE MOVEMENTS

1. Embrace a Reparative Perspective on Health:

- Spend time researching and understanding the concept of disease as a reparative process, exploring various sources to deepen your knowledge.
- Engage in discussions or online forums to share and exchange perspectives on this alternative view of health and disease.
- Challenge yourself to reframe your thinking when encountering health challenges, viewing them as potential reparative processes rather than solely negative experiences.

2. Integrate Hygiene and Health Practices:

- Dedicate time each day for thorough handwashing and personal hygiene, ensuring you follow recommended guidelines to minimize the risk of infections.
- Create a weekly cleaning schedule for your living space, including disinfecting commonly used surfaces and frequently touched items.
- Explore natural cleaning products or homemade solutions to maintain a clean environment while minimizing exposure to harsh chemicals.

3. Explore Probiotics and Gut Health:

- Research the role of probiotics and beneficial bacteria in promoting gut health and overall well-being.
- Incorporate probiotic-rich foods into your diet, such as yogurt, kefir, sauerkraut, kimchi,

or kombucha, aiming for at least one serving per day.

- Consider consulting a healthcare professional before introducing any significant changes to your diet, especially if you have specific health concerns.

4. Balance Medical Interventions and Natural Healing:

- When facing a health issue, engage in thoughtful discussions with healthcare professionals to understand both medical interventions and potential natural healing processes.
- Seek a second opinion or explore alternative treatment options to ensure you're making informed decisions about your health.
- Educate yourself on potential side effects of medications and their impact on the body's natural healing mechanisms, making well-informed choices in consultation with your healthcare provider.

5. Reflect on Microbial Interconnectedness:

- Engage in gardening or composting to foster a deeper understanding of the role of microorganisms in decomposition and nutrient cycling.
- Explore educational resources or documentaries that delve into the intricate relationships between microorganisms, nature, and human health.
- Consider participating in local environmental or conservation initiatives to actively contribute to preserving and understanding the delicate balance of microbial life in ecosystems.

By taking these actionable steps, you can actively incorporate the insights from the chapter into your daily life, promoting a more holistic and informed approach to health and well-being.

Record your reflections, insights, and observations on the concepts discussed earlier.

Use this space to brainstorm, sketch, or jot down any questions that arise in your mind. Make it a truly personal experience.

CHAPTER 3: FAMILIARISING WITH A FUNGUS FEAST

Summary

The chapter delves into the characteristics of fungi, their dietary preferences, and their impact on human health. Fungi, as living microorganisms, require food to grow and thrive. There are approximately 1.5 million different types of fungi, and while their preferences may vary, they all share a penchant for sugar in its various forms.

Fungi's favorite food is sugar, particularly the concentrated form extracted from sugar cane or sugar beet plants. However, if denied this source, fungi can also thrive on alternatives such as honey, maple syrup, and sugars found in fruits. The consumption of certain foods can encourage fungal growth in the body. Alcoholic beverages contain mycotoxins and yeast, yeast breads contribute to fungal growth, and foods like peanuts and cooked rice are highly susceptible to mold. Additionally, foods containing yeast or molds, such as brewer's yeast, yeast extract spreads, and mushrooms, can promote fungal growth and should be limited.

The chapter highlights how fungal evolution occurs within the human body due to unhealthy lifestyle habits leading to cell damage. This prompts microorganisms, initially bacteria, to adapt and clean up cellular waste. With continued unhealthy habits and the abundance of added sugars in modern diets, these microorganisms can evolve into yeast and fungi, which can produce toxic waste contributing to disease. Fungal invasion into the human body can occur through ingestion of moldy food or antibiotics, inhalation of mold spores, skin penetration, and even sexual transmission. The presence of a favorable food supply, often high in sugar, enables the survival and proliferation of fungal spores. Severe cases of invasion can lead to rapid and dangerous fungal growth, potentially resulting in death.

The chapter further defines the role of fungi in the human body's ecosystem. Fungi play a crucial role as "exterminators," breaking down dead and decaying matter where cell damage or death occurs. It also discusses how chemicals, synthetic hormones, and heavy metals can contribute to fungal growth. Chemicals from various sources, including non-organic foods and household products, provide a food supply for opportunistic microorganisms. Synthetic hormones, like estrogen, can lead to rapid yeast and fungal multiplication. Heavy metals, such as mercury, which accumulate in the body, can also serve as a food source for fungi.

The chapter concludes by highlighting the need for alternatives and healthier practices to combat fungal growth. It emphasizes the importance of balanced hormone levels, reducing exposure to environmental toxins, and considering alternatives to harmful practices like mercury dental fillings.

DEFINING THE FUNGI PALLET IN THE HUMAN BODY

The concept of defining the fungal palette within the human body encompasses three key aspects: waste management, chemical exposure, synthetic hormones, and heavy metals.

Waste Management: Fungi, acting as nature's cleaners, play a role in removing deceased and decaying matter from the environment. In the human body, wherever there is cell damage or death, microorganisms like bacteria, fungi, and yeast are present to aid in the cleanup process.

Chemical Exposure: The introduction of new chemicals each year, including those present in herbicides, insecticides, and pesticides, has led to the accumulation of residues in non-organically grown produce like fruits, vegetables, nuts, and grains. Common sources of contamination also include meat, poultry, fish, dairy products, and eggs. Additionally, toxic chemicals are found in various household items such as cleaning products, laundry detergents, soaps, shampoos, toothpaste, perfumes, and makeup. Synthetic fibers like nylon, acrylic, and polyester release chemicals that can be absorbed by the skin, especially when perspiring. These environmental toxins generate harmful free radicals that damage living tissue, creating a food source for opportunistic microorganisms like bacteria, yeast, and fungi.

Synthetic Hormones: Synthetic hormones, often present in contraceptives and hormone replacement therapies, typically contain estrogen. Estrogen's role as a cell proliferator triggers significant cell growth. Elevated estrogen levels can accelerate the multiplication of yeast and fungi. Various authors, including Dr. John Lee, Dr. Sandra Cabot, and Dr. Sherrill Sellman, have authored valuable guides on natural hormone balance. While natural birth control methods offered by Family Planning Clinics present an alternative to hormonal contraceptives, they may be less convenient but certainly less life-threatening.

Heavy Metals: Metal amalgam fillings, composed of up to 40-60% mercury, have been utilized in dentistry for the past five decades. Over time, this mercury is absorbed by the body and accumulates as methyl mercury, the most toxic form. Mercury is known to have neurotoxic effects, and no safe dose exists for humans. Fungi, proficient at breaking down heavy metals in soil, can also thrive on heavy metal accumulations in human tissues. Safer alternatives to mercury fillings are now available, offering comparable strength without the same toxicity, and often boasting cosmetic advantages.

In conclusion, defining the fungal palette within the human body involves recognizing the roles fungi play in waste management, understanding the impact of chemical exposure on fungal proliferation, acknowledging the influence of synthetic hormones on yeast and fungal growth, and appreciating the interaction between fungi and heavy metals. By comprehending these relationships, individuals can make informed decisions to manage their health and reduce the risks associated with fungal overgrowth and its potential consequences.

LESSONS AND KEY POINTS FROM THIS CHAPTER

1. **Fungi as Living Microorganisms:** Fungi are distinct microorganisms neither belonging to the plant nor animal kingdom. They require food for growth and are estimated to comprise around 1.5 million different types. Despite variations, their shared preference for sugar is a key characteristic.

2. **Sugar as Fungi's Favorite Food:** Fungi thrive on sugar, particularly concentrated forms derived from sugar cane or sugar beet plants. Honey, maple syrup, and fruit sugars are alternative sources. Certain foods, including alcoholic beverages, yeasty breads, peanuts, and rice, encourage fungal growth. Foods containing yeast or molds, like brewer's yeast and mushrooms, also contribute to this.

3. **Fungal Evolution and Impact:** Unhealthy lifestyle habits can lead to cell damage, triggering fungal evolution. Microorganisms like bacteria initially adapt to cleanse cellular waste, but excessive sugar consumption can lead to the evolution of yeast and fungi. These microorganisms produce toxic waste, contributing to disease.

4. **Modes of Fungal Invasion:** Fungal invasion into the body can occur through ingesting moldy food, antibiotics, inhalation of mold spores, skin penetration, or sexual transmission. A high-sugar diet provides a favorable environment for fungal survival, potentially leading to severe and rapid growth.

5. **Fungi's Role in Waste Management:** Fungi act as "exterminators," breaking down dead matter in nature. Similarly, in the human body, where cell damage or death occurs, microorganisms such as bacteria, fungi, and yeast aid in cleanup.

6. **Impact of Chemical Exposure:** Introduction of new chemicals, like herbicides and pesticides, accumulates residues in non-organic produce and various products. Toxic

chemicals found in household items release harmful free radicals, damaging living tissue, which can serve as a food source for opportunistic microorganisms.

7. **Synthetic Hormones and Fungal Growth:** Synthetic hormones, notably estrogen, present in contraceptives and hormone therapies, promote rapid cell growth. Elevated estrogen levels lead to increased yeast and fungal multiplication.

8. **Heavy Metals and Fungal Interaction:** Metal amalgam fillings containing mercury accumulate in human tissues. Fungi, proficient at breaking down heavy metals in soil, can also feed on heavy metal accumulations in the body. Safer alternatives to mercury fillings exist.

9. **Holistic Health Considerations:** The chapter emphasizes balanced hormone levels, reduced exposure to environmental toxins, and alternative practices to combat fungal growth. It underscores the importance of understanding fungal interactions for informed health decisions.

REFLECTION QUESTIONS

1. Dietary Impact and Awareness: How does understanding fungi's preference for sugar and its various forms influence your dietary choices? Are there specific changes you could make to reduce sugar intake and potentially discourage fungal growth?

2. Personal Health Habits: Reflect on your lifestyle habits. Are there areas where you could improve to reduce cell damage and the potential for fungal evolution? How might you strike a balance between enjoying life while maintaining a healthier environment for your body's microorganisms?

3. Chemical Exposure and Toxin Awareness: How conscious are you of the chemicals present in your daily life, including in foods, household products, and personal care items? Are there steps you could take to minimize your exposure and reduce the potential for creating an environment conducive to fungal growth?

4. Hormonal Balance and Health: Consider the role of synthetic hormones and their impact on yeast and fungal multiplication. Are you aware of natural approaches to hormonal balance? How might you integrate holistic practices into your routine to promote hormonal health?

5. Holistic Health Decision-Making: Given the interplay between fungi, diet, chemicals, hormones, and heavy metals, how does this chapter's information influence your overall approach to health decisions? What steps could you take to create a more balanced and harmonious environment within your body?

MILESTONE GOALS

Healthier Lifestyle Choices: To gain a comprehensive understanding of how fungi interact with the human body and influence health, with the aim of making informed dietary and lifestyle choices that minimize fungal growth and promote overall well-being. This goal involves learning about the types of foods that encourage fungal growth, understanding the impact of chemicals and synthetic hormones, and identifying strategies to reduce exposure to environmental toxins.

Balanced Hormonal Health: To grasp the connection between synthetic hormones, fungal multiplication, and hormonal balance, with the intention of exploring natural methods to regulate hormones and prevent excessive yeast and fungal growth. Achieving this goal involves delving into the role of synthetic hormones, learning about authors and resources that discuss natural hormone balance, and considering alternative approaches to contraceptives and hormone therapies.

Safer Dental Practices: To become aware of the potential risks associated with heavy metal exposure, particularly mercury from dental fillings, and to explore alternative dental options to safeguard health. This goal includes understanding the dangers of heavy metal accumulation, researching safer dental filling alternatives, and potentially taking steps to replace existing mercury fillings for both health and cosmetic reasons.

ACTIONABLE MOVEMENTS

1. Mindful Sugar Consumption and Dietary Choices:

- Label Scrutiny: Dedicate time to examining nutrition labels on packaged foods. Aim to choose products with minimal added sugars, and opt for whole-food options whenever possible.
- Creative Alternatives: Experiment with baking or cooking using natural sweeteners like honey or maple syrup instead of refined sugar. Try a new recipe that features these alternatives.
- Daily Sugar Audit: For one day this week, track your sugar intake using a mobile app or journal. Reflect on your findings and identify opportunities to reduce sugar consumption.

2. Reducing Chemical Exposure and Environmental Toxins:

- Green Cleaning: Research and prepare a homemade, eco-friendly cleaning solution using simple ingredients like vinegar, baking soda, and essential oils. Use it to clean a commonly used area in your home.
- Toxin-Free Day: Choose a specific day this week to go entirely chemical-free in terms of personal care products. Use natural alternatives for skincare, haircare, and cosmetics.
- Natural Freshness: Experiment with a natural method for keeping your home smelling fresh, such as using essential oil diffusers or simmering a pot of water with citrus peels and herbs.

3. Hormonal Balance and Natural Health Practices:

- Holistic Self-Care Routine: Design a daily self-care routine that incorporates natural elements like herbal teas, gentle yoga stretches. Commit to following this routine for at least three days this week.
- Hormone-Balancing Meal: Plan and prepare a hormone-balancing meal that includes ingredients like cruciferous vegetables, flaxseeds, and lean protein sources.
- Reflective Journaling: Spend 15 minutes each day reflecting on your hormonal health journey. Note any changes you observe in your energy levels, mood, or overall well-being.

Record your reflections, insights, and observations on the concepts discussed earlier.

Use this space to brainstorm, sketch, or jot down any questions that arise in your mind. Make it a truly personal experience.

CHAPTER 4: MYCOLOGY
THE STUDY OF FUNGI

Summary

The exploration of mycology commenced with the groundbreaking discovery of aflatoxin in the early 1960s. Skin leprosy, however, is understood as an infectious skin disease, although previous translation norms would suggest interpreting it as skin mildew.

Mycotoxins, the toxic byproducts of fungi, have been well-documented contributors to diseases across plants, animals, and humans. The precise count of mycotoxins remains uncertain, potentially numbering in the millions due to the diverse array of toxic metabolites generated by fungi. These mycotoxins, produced by yeasts, fungi, and molds, are akin to the "urine and feces" of these organisms, resulting from their consumption of nutrients. These toxic substances are designed to eliminate competitors for the fungi's food source, and specific mycotoxins can even act as virulence factors in inducing diseases in various organisms.

The American Council of Agricultural Science and Technology (CAST) acknowledges the challenge of quantifying the economic impact of mycotoxins. Their rough estimate, which dates back to 2003, suggested annual losses of around $932 million solely in the US due to mycotoxin-related food and stock feed damages, a figure likely to have increased over time.

In Australia, where nearly 90 percent of the population resides in urban areas, the necessity for substantial food production and storage is prominent. This situation has led to an issue with fungal infections in stored grains, particularly in moisture-prone silos. Corn, wheat, and peanuts are commonly affected by mold and fungal growth in such environments.

Among the most frequently identified disease-causing mycotoxins in foods are those produced by potentially toxic fungal species such as Aspergillus, Penicillium, and Fusarium. These include Aflatoxin, Ochratoxin, Trichothecenes, Zearalenone, Fumonisin, Citreoviridum, Penicillic acid, and Gliotoxin. Notably, Aflatoxin is considered one of the most carcinogenic substances ever tested, with documented links to hepatocellular carcinoma and other cancers in different parts of the world. Kwashiorkor and Reye's syndrome are also associated with aflatoxin contamination.

Research has uncovered connections between mycotoxins and various diseases. Aflatoxin, for instance, has been detected in the liver tissue of children with Kwashiorkor and associated with liver cancer. Ochratoxin primarily impacts the kidneys but can also affect the liver, linking it to diseases like Balkan Endemic Nephropathy. Trichothecenes, known for their potent protein inhibition properties, have caused severe gastrointestinal distress. Zearalenone has been linked to premature puberty and cervical cancer, while Fumonisin is correlated with esophageal cancer rates in certain regions.

Citreoviridum, identified as the cause of historical acute cardiac beriberi, experienced a decline with reduced exposure to moldy rice. Gliotoxin, initially investigated for antibiotic potential, was rediscovered for its immunosuppressive attributes and found in vaginal secretions. Its role in the pathogenesis of infections like Aspergillosis and Candidiasis could be significant due to its immunosuppressive nature.

In conclusion, mycology's origin story dates back to the revelation of aflatoxin, and fungal diseases have been known for centuries. Mycotoxins, toxic metabolites produced by fungi, contribute to diseases in diverse organisms. Their economic impact is substantial, with estimations of significant losses. Urbanization in countries like Australia has exacerbated the challenge of maintaining fungal-free food storage. Specific mycotoxins from fungi like Aspergillus, Penicillium, and Fusarium have been implicated in various diseases, underscoring the importance of understanding and managing these health risks.

LESSONS AND KEY POINTS FROM THIS CHAPTER

1. Historical Roots of Mycology: Mycology originated with the discovery of aflatoxin in the 1960s, but references to fungal-related diseases can be found in ancient texts such as the Bible.

2. Mycotoxins and Disease: Mycotoxins, toxic waste products of fungi, have been documented to cause diseases in plants, animals, and humans. The true number of mycotoxins remains unknown, but their diversity could potentially reach into the millions.

3. **Mycotoxin Production:** Mycotoxins are produced by yeast, fungi, and molds during their consumption of nutrients. These toxins are essentially the metabolic waste of fungi and serve to eliminate competing organisms for resources.

4. **Virulence Factors:** Certain mycotoxins function as potential virulence factors, enhancing the ability of fungi to cause diseases in various organisms.

5. **Economic Impact:** Estimating the precise economic cost of mycotoxins is challenging. The American Council of Agricultural Science and Technology (CAST) suggests a rough estimate of $932 million in annual food and stock feed losses in the US due to mycotoxin contamination, a figure that has likely increased over time.

6. **Urbanization and Food Storage:** With the majority of Australians living in urban areas, large-scale food production and storage are necessary. This situation has contributed to the emergence of issues related to fungal infections in stored grains, such as corn, wheat, and peanuts.

7. **Common Mycotoxins:** Aspergillus, Penicillium, and Fusarium are common fungal species that produce potentially toxic mycotoxins in grains. These include Aflatoxin, Ochratoxin, Trichothecenes, Zearalenone, Fumonisin, Citreoviridum, Penicillic acid, and Gliotoxin.

8. **Aflatoxin's Carcinogenicity:** Aflatoxin is regarded as one of the most carcinogenic substances tested, with links to hepatocellular carcinoma (liver cancer) and gastrointestinal tract and liver cancers.

9. **Health Impacts:** Mycotoxins have been implicated in various health conditions. Aflatoxin has been detected in the liver tissue of children with Kwashiorkor and is associated with liver cancer. Ochratoxin primarily affects the kidneys, Trichothecenes cause severe gastrointestinal symptoms, Zearalenone is linked to premature puberty and cervical cancer, and Fumonisin is correlated with esophageal cancer.

10. **Citreoviridum and Beriberi:** Citreoviridum was identified as the cause of acute cardiac beriberi, a historical disease characterized by a rapid pulse, vomiting, and low blood pressure. Its incidence decreased with reduced exposure to moldy rice.

11. **Immunosuppressive Gliotoxin:** Gliotoxin, initially studied for antibiotic potential, is known for its immunosuppressive properties. It has been found in vaginal secretions and could play a role in infections like Aspergillosis and Candidiasis.

REFLECTION QUESTIONS

Have you ever considered the historical origins of scientific fields and discoveries? How does learning about the early days of mycology impact your perspective on its modern significance?

Are you aware of the diverse range of mycotoxins and their impacts on different organisms? How might this awareness influence your views on food safety and regulation?

Do you find the analogy of mycotoxins as the "urine and feces" of fungi intriguing? How does this perspective on fungal metabolism deepen your appreciation for the intricate interactions between fungi and their environment?

Considering the concept of mycotoxins as potential virulence factors, how might this change your perception of fungal diseases and the strategies used by fungi to thrive in different host organisms?

How does learning about the specific health impacts of mycotoxins influence your thoughts on disease prevention, public health initiatives, and personal health choices?

_____

_____

_____

MILESTONE GOALS

1. Understand the Historical Significance of Mycology and Fungal Diseases:
Goal: Gain an appreciation for the historical context and origins of mycology, as well as the presence of fungal-related illnesses throughout history.

2. Identify Key Mycotoxins and Their Health Implications:
Goal: Learn about different mycotoxins, their sources, and their potential impact on human health, including their role in various diseases such as cancer and kidney-related issues.

3. Recognize the Economic and Practical Implications of Fungal Diseases:
Goal: Comprehend the economic challenges posed by mycotoxin-related damages, especially in the context of agriculture and food production. Understand the practical difficulties posed by fungal infections in stored grains and the importance of managing these issues.

ACTIONABLE MOVEMENTS

1. Improve Food Storage and Consumption Practices:

- Check your pantry and storage areas for signs of mold or fungal growth regularly.
- Invest in airtight containers for storing grains, nuts, and other susceptible foods.
- Rotate your food stock regularly to ensure older items are used first.
- Avoid purchasing bulk quantities of grains or nuts that might not be consumed quickly.
- Be mindful of food expiration dates and properly discard expired items.

2. Enhance Food Safety in Urban Settings:

- If you live in an urban area, research local food sources, such as farmers' markets, to access fresher produce.
- Consider participating in community gardens or supporting local agriculture initiatives to have more control over your food sources.

- Educate yourself about food safety practices specific to urban environments, such as proper storage and handling of produce.

3. Support Research and Health Advocacy:

- Look for local or international organizations focused on mycology research or food safety education, and consider volunteering or donating to support their efforts.
- Stay informed about regulations and policies related to mycotoxin control in your country.
- Share the knowledge from the chapter with friends, family, or social networks to raise awareness about mycotoxin-related health risks.
- Remember, actionable movements should be specific, achievable steps that you can integrate into your routine to make a positive impact based on the information you've gained from the chapter.

Record your reflections, insights, and observations on the concepts discussed earlier.

Use this space to brainstorm, sketch, or jot down any questions that arise in your mind. Make it a truly personal experience.

CHAPTER 5:
PRESENTING THE EVIDENCE, HISTORY OF FUNGUS
THE ROLE FUNGUS PLAYS IN HUMAN DISEASE

Summary

In this chapter, the author discusses the process of dealing with a house affected by mildew, which is considered dangerous and deadly according to historical context. The process involves removing the stones with mildew from the house, scraping the house's interior, replacing the stones, and plastering them in. If the mildew returns, the house is declared unclean and destroyed, with remnants taken to an unclean area outside the city.

The chapter then transitions into discussing the connection between mildew and disease, particularly focusing on the role of fungi in human ailments. It highlights the Hebrew word for leprosy being used for both skin conditions and house contamination. Modern translations use the term "mildew" for houses and clothes but not for skin issues, replacing it with "infectious skin disease."

The narrative shifts to contemporary scientific understanding, where more doctors and scientists are discovering the fungal link to various diseases, reflecting historical beliefs. The chapter emphasizes the work of Dr. Milton White, who explored the connection between fungi and disease, particularly cancer. Dr. White's research revealed that certain fungal spores were involved in causing cancer, and they could transform inside a human host, invading cells and reproducing.

The chapter delves into the concept of pleomorphism, which describes the changing roles of microbes in the human body. While conventional medicine largely follows Louis Pasteur's monomorphism theory (microbes stay in one form), several scientists like Professor Gunther

Enderlein, Antoine Bechamp, Claude Bernard, and Royal Raymond Rife demonstrated that microbes can change roles based on the body's conditions.

The account explores various scientific findings that highlight the pleomorphic nature of microorganisms. It discusses how microscopic life forms can change roles from builders to destroyers of cells and adapt to the body's internal environment, known as "The Terrain." Researchers like Dr. Virginia Livingston discovered pleomorphic organisms in cancer and demonstrated how they could be dormant or activated based on the body's needs.

The chapter also mentions studies by Ida H. Mattman, Florence Seibert, Sorin Sonea, and Maurice Parisset that confirm bacterial pleomorphism as a scientific fact. It explains that these microorganisms change forms depending on the medium they grow in and their duration of growth. The chapter further connects this phenomenon to the Carbon Cycle, where microorganisms play a crucial role in breaking down organic matter.

The narrative concludes by emphasizing the role of fungi, yeast, and mold as "undertakers" in the Carbon Cycle, breaking down organic material and preventing the planet from being covered in waste. It cites the medical textbook "Principles and Practice of Clinical Mycology," which outlines the fungal link to human diseases in detail.

Overall, this chapter presents a historical account of dealing with mildew-contaminated houses, bridges it to a modern scientific understanding of fungal links to diseases, and explores the concept of pleomorphism to illustrate the dynamic nature of microorganisms in the human body and their role in the Carbon Cycle.

LESSONS AND KEY POINTS FROM THIS CHAPTER

1. Historical Practices: The chapter highlights the historical practices of dealing with mildew-contaminated houses, shedding light on the ancient belief that mildew was considered dangerous and deadly. This reflects the significance of cleanliness and hygiene in ancient societies.

2. Mildew and Disease: The discussion of the Hebrew word for leprosy being used for both skin conditions and house contamination points to the historical belief in a connection between mildew and disease, even though modern translations differentiate between the two contexts.

3. Fungal Link to Diseases: The chapter emphasizes that the modern scientific community is increasingly recognizing the fungal link to various diseases. The work of Dr. Milton White and his findings regarding the involvement of fungal spores in cancer highlights the importance of understanding the role of fungi in disease development.

4. Pleomorphism: The concept of pleomorphism is a central theme, indicating that microbes can change roles based on the body's conditions. This contrasts with the traditional monomorphism theory that states microbes remain in fixed forms. The historical and contemporary examples of scientists like Antoine Bechamp, Claude Bernard, and others illustrate the dynamic nature of microorganisms.

5. The Terrain and Microorganisms: Claude Bernard's concept of "The Terrain" emphasizes that the internal environment of the body plays a crucial role in determining disease conditions, more so than the microorganisms themselves. This underscores the importance of overall bodily health in disease prevention.

6. Microorganisms and Cancer: Researchers like Dr. Virginia Livingston's discovery of pleomorphic organisms in all cancers studied, and their potential role in cell repair and activation, suggest a deeper understanding of how microorganisms might influence cancer development and progression.

7. Carbon Cycle and Microorganisms: The chapter explains the connection between pleomorphism and the Carbon Cycle. It underscores that microorganisms play a fundamental role in breaking down organic matter, showcasing how they are both builders and decomposers in the cycle of life and death.

8. Scientific Shift: The chapter shows a shift in scientific understanding from rigid monomorphism to a more flexible view of pleomorphism, which has implications for how diseases are understood, treated, and prevented.

9. Microscopic Study: The work of researchers like Royal Raymond Rife, Sorin Sonea, and Maurice Parisset, who employed advanced microscopic techniques, demonstrates how observing microorganisms at different stages of growth can yield valuable insights into their adaptive behavior.

10. Role of Fungi: Fungi, yeast, and mold play essential roles as "undertakers" in the Carbon Cycle, breaking down organic material and returning it to the earth. This natural process is vital for maintaining ecological balance.

11. Carbon Cycle as a Metaphor: The chapter uses the Carbon Cycle as a metaphor to highlight the cyclical nature of life, change, and transformation, applying it to both the microbial world and larger ecological processes.

REFLECTION QUESTIONS

In the context of disease prevention and health, how has your understanding evolved from viewing microorganisms as fixed entities to recognizing their dynamic and adaptable nature, as discussed in the chapter?

Reflect on the concept of "The Terrain" proposed by Claude Bernard. How does this idea align with modern holistic approaches to health and disease prevention? How might it influence your own health choices?

Have you ever experienced a situation where your body's internal environment (terrain) played a significant role in your health outcomes? How might understanding the dynamic nature of microorganisms impact your approach to health management?

Think about pleomorphism and the idea that microorganisms can change roles. Can you draw any parallels between this concept and personal growth or adaptability in various life circumstances?

The Carbon Cycle metaphor suggests a cyclical pattern of growth, decay, and renewal in both the microbial world and nature at large. How might you apply this metaphor to personal challenges, transformations, or your understanding of life's cycles?

Think about the concept of adapting your environment to support habits. How can you apply this principle to your daily routine or goals, particularly in the context of health, learning, or personal development?

_____

_____

_____

MILESTONE GOALS

Enhance Health Awareness.

Goal: Develop a deeper understanding of the fungal link to diseases and the role of microorganisms in human health.

Adapt a Holistic Approach to Well-being.

Goal: Embrace the concept of "The Terrain" and its influence on health outcomes, and apply this holistic perspective to your own well-being.

Foster Personal Growth through Adaptability.

Goal: Embrace the concept of pleomorphism and apply its principles to personal growth and adaptability in various life circumstances.

ACTIONABLE MOVEMENTS

1. House Maintenance and Health Protection:
- If you encounter mildew or mold growth in your home, consider taking immediate action to remove affected stones, thoroughly clean the interior, and replace the stones.
- Regularly inspect and address any signs of mildew or fungal growth in your living environment, as it can have negative health implications.

2. Understanding Fungal Infections:

- Be aware of the connection between fungi and diseases, not just in houses but also in human ailments. Understanding this link can help you take precautions and seek appropriate medical attention if needed.
- Stay informed about the historical context of diseases like leprosy and how they were associated with both skin conditions and environmental contamination.

3. Awareness of Pleomorphism:

- Familiarize yourself with the concept of pleomorphism in microorganisms. While conventional wisdom follows the monomorphism theory, exploring the idea that microbes can change roles based on conditions could have implications for healthcare and disease management.

4. Holistic Health Approach:

- Recognize the importance of considering the body's internal environment or "The Terrain" when addressing health issues. This holistic approach can guide medical treatments and lifestyle choices.

5. Scientific Discoveries:

- Stay updated on scientific research related to fungal links to diseases. Understanding how certain microorganisms can transform and impact health can lead to better health management strategies.

6. Environmental Impact:

- Acknowledge the role of microorganisms, particularly fungi, yeast, and mold, in the Carbon Cycle. Recognize their contribution as "undertakers" in breaking down organic material, thereby helping to prevent waste accumulation and supporting ecosystem health.

7. Personal Health Choices:

- Incorporate awareness of fungal connections to diseases into your lifestyle choices. This might involve dietary considerations, environmental hygiene, and seeking medical advice for persistent health issues.

8. Sustainable Practices:

- Reflect on the role of microorganisms in the Carbon Cycle and their impact on waste decomposition. Consider adopting sustainable practices that align with nature's recycling mechanisms to reduce waste generation.

9. Educational Pursuits:

- If interested, explore further into the research of scientists like Dr. Milton White, Dr. Virginia Livingston, and others who have contributed to understanding the relationship between microorganisms and diseases. This knowledge could inform healthcare practices.

Record your reflections, insights, and observations on the concepts discussed earlier.

Use this space to brainstorm, sketch, or jot down any questions that arise in your mind. Make it a truly personal experience.

CHAPTER 6:
THE LINK BETWEEN
FUNGUS AND CANCER

Summary

The chapter discusses the historical research and evidence linking fungal infections with diseases, particularly cancer. It highlights the work of various researchers and medical professionals who have explored this connection.

The chapter begins by acknowledging the long-standing research that has established a link between fungi and various diseases throughout the last century. It then delves into the compelling evidence connecting fungi and cancer over the past few decades.

Professor A.V. Constantine, a former head of the World Health Organization's Department of Mycology, is mentioned for his contributions. He has written books that provide documentary evidence showing the relationship between fungi, their metabolites (mycotoxins), and degenerative and cancerous diseases. Doug Kaufmann, another researcher, has written books demonstrating the connection between fungi and diseases, including various cancers. His book "The Germ That Causes Cancer" reveals that the link between fungus and cancer has been recognized for over a century.

Dr. Tullio Simoncini's work is highlighted, as he published the book "Cancer is a Fungus: A revolution in the therapy of tumours" in 2007. He proposes that candida, a type of fungus, is the cause of cancer and suggests treating cancer with a simple, safe, and inexpensive method—sodium bicarbonate. He explains that sodium bicarbonate's alkalinity disrupts the cancer cells' environment by allowing oxygen to enter, which is detrimental to cancer cells. Additionally, it eliminates the organic materials that fungi use for nourishment.

Dr. Simoncini's treatment involves applying sodium bicarbonate locally, with catheters used for hard-to-reach areas. He emphasizes the importance of evaluating the patient's emotional well-being, along with proper hydration and diet.

The chapter shifts to discussing the findings of Dr. T. Colin Campbell's book "The China Study," which explores nutrition and its effects on health. Campbell's research focuses on the link between diet, particularly protein consumption, and cancer. He found that high animal protein consumption correlated with a higher risk of liver cancer, while low-protein diets or plant protein did not promote cancer growth. The chapter notes the significance of this research in understanding the relationship between diet and cancer risk.

The chapter also touches on Dr. Otto Warburg's work in the 20th century, where he discovered that cancer cells function anaerobically, without oxygen. This discovery supports the idea that cancer cells thrive in acidic environments.

The chapter concludes by reevaluating conventional medical cancer treatments. It questions the effectiveness and side effects of chemotherapy, as well as the impact of cytotoxic chemotherapy on survival rates in various malignancies.

Overall, the chapter provides a comprehensive overview of the evidence connecting fungal infections, diet, and cancer, while also questioning the effectiveness of certain medical treatments. It highlights the contributions of multiple researchers and their findings in this area.

Experienced oncologists, explore the effectiveness of cancer treatments, primarily focusing on chemotherapy, radiotherapy, and surgery. The lead author, Associate Professor Graeme Morgan, works as a radiation oncologist at Royal North Shore Hospital in Sydney. Professor Robyn Ward is a medical oncologist at the University of New South Wales and Saint Vincent's Hospital. Additionally, Professor Ward is associated with the Therapeutic Goods Authority of the Australian Federal Departments of Health and Ageing, an official body that evaluates drugs for inclusion on the national Pharmaceutical Benefits Schedule (PBS). The third author, Doctor Michael Barton, is a radiation oncologist and a member of the Collaboration for Cancer Outcomes Research and Evaluation, Liverpool Health Service, Sydney.

The core findings of this chapter are based on a comprehensive analysis of randomized controlled clinical trials (RCTs) conducted in Australia and the US, covering the time span from January 1990 to January 2004. The authors particularly focused on RCTs that demonstrated a statistically significant increase in 5-year survival due to the use of chemotherapy in treating adult malignancies. They gathered survival data from Australian cancer registries and the US National Cancer Institute's Surveillance Epidemiology and

End Results (SEER) registry. To ensure their analysis erred on the side of caution, they intentionally overestimated the benefits of chemotherapy wherever data were unclear.

The key conclusion of the authors' meticulous study is that chemotherapy contributes slightly more than 2 percent to the improvement of survival rates in cancer patients. The chapter then delves into the discussions of other cancer treatment methods: radiotherapy and surgery.

Radiotherapy, as a method of burning out cancer cells, presents challenges due to its tendency to damage surrounding tissues and organs. These damaged tissues can become susceptible to opportunistic fungal infections. While radiotherapy may initially lead to regression in cancer growth, it can paradoxically create an environment conducive to cancer's resurgence.

Surgery, on the other hand, involves cutting the body, which results in damage and a potentially favorable environment for fungal growth. The chapter mentions that in some cases, particularly when a tumor is large and can be safely removed, benefits might arise from surgical intervention, combined with washing the area with sodium bicarbonate.

However, the underlying argument in the chapter is that these traditional treatments—chemotherapy, radiotherapy, and surgery—often fail to address the root causes of cancer. These methods are considered dangerous and involve significant risks. The authors point out that such treatments, which involve burning, poisoning, and slashing the body, contradict the natural healing mechanisms of the body. The authors call for exploring and investigating alternatives that align with the body's inherent healing powers. The chapter concludes with a suggestion that, in the future, the current trend of cancer treatments might be seen as barbaric, similar to how bloodletting is viewed today. This suggests a potential shift towards more holistic and less invasive approaches to cancer treatment.

LESSONS AND KEY POINTS FROM THIS CHAPTER

1. Historical Research Linking Fungal Infections and Diseases: The chapter acknowledges the longstanding research connecting fungi with various diseases over the last century, setting the foundation for discussing the link between fungi and cancer.

2. Evidence of Fungi-Cancer Connection: The chapter highlights compelling evidence from recent decades that suggests a relationship between fungal infections and cancer. It explores the work of researchers who have explored this connection.

3. Contributions of Notable Researchers: The chapter profiles researchers like Professor A.V. Constantine, Doug Kaufmann, and Dr. Tullio Simoncini, who have contributed to understanding the link between fungi and cancer. Simoncini's work suggests treating cancer with sodium bicarbonate to disrupt the fungal environment.

4. Diet and Cancer Link: Dr. T. Colin Campbell's research in "The China Study" highlights the correlation between high animal protein consumption and increased cancer risk. This underscores the importance of diet in cancer prevention.

5. Warburg Effect and Acidic Environments: Dr. Otto Warburg's discovery that cancer cells function anaerobically in the absence of oxygen supports the idea that cancer cells thrive in acidic environments.

6. Reevaluation of Conventional Cancer Treatments: The chapter questions the effectiveness and side effects of chemotherapy, as well as the impact of cytotoxic chemotherapy on survival rates. It encourages critical thinking about traditional treatments.

7. Authors and Study Overview: The authors, experienced oncologists, conducted a comprehensive analysis of randomized controlled clinical trials (RCTs) in Australia and the US between 1990 and 2004. They focused on chemotherapy's contribution to survival rates.

8. Chemotherapy's Limited Impact on Survival: The authors' study concludes that chemotherapy contributes slightly more than 2 percent to the improvement of survival rates in cancer patients. This challenges the notion of chemotherapy as a primary solution.

9. Radiotherapy's Challenges: Radiotherapy's damage to surrounding tissues and susceptibility to opportunistic fungal infections are discussed. The paradoxical environment it can create for cancer's resurgence is highlighted.

10. Surgery and Fungal Growth: Surgery's potential to create a favorable environment for fungal growth is mentioned. However, in certain cases, surgical intervention combined with sodium bicarbonate washing might be beneficial.

11. Addressing Root Causes of Cancer: The core argument is that traditional treatments often fail to address the root causes of cancer. Such treatments are considered risky and counterproductive to the body's natural healing mechanisms.

12. Call for Holistic Approaches: The authors advocate for exploring alternatives that align with the body's inherent healing powers. The chapter concludes by suggesting a potential shift towards more holistic and less invasive approaches to cancer treatment.

REFLECTION QUESTIONS

Do you believe that historical research can offer valuable insights into present-day medical practices?

_____

_____

_____

Have you ever encountered information that challenged conventional medical treatments? How open are you to considering alternative approaches?

_____

_____

_____

In what ways do you think your diet might contribute to your overall health and the prevention of diseases, including cancer?

_____

_____

_____

Reflecting on your own health habits, do you think you are more influenced by societal norms or by evidence-based research?

_____

_____

_____

Considering the discussion about the impact of the environment on health, what changes could you make to your surroundings to support healthier habits?

_____

_____

_____

MILESTONE GOALS

1. Gain a Comprehensive Understanding of the Fungi-Cancer Connection

- Read and analyze the chapter to comprehend the historical research and evidence linking fungal infections to diseases, particularly cancer.
- Extract key findings about the contributions of researchers and their work in establishing this connection.
- Synthesize the presented evidence to develop a clear understanding of the potential link between fungi and cancer.

2. Evaluate Traditional Cancer Treatments and Explore Alternative Approaches

- Critically examine the chapter's discussions on the effectiveness and limitations of chemotherapy, radiotherapy, and surgery in treating cancer.
- Reflect on the challenges and risks associated with these conventional treatments and their impact on survival rates.
- Explore the chapter's suggestions for holistic and less invasive approaches to cancer treatment, considering the potential benefits of aligning with the body's natural healing mechanisms.

3. Consider the Role of Diet and Environment in Health and Disease Prevention

- Analyze the chapter's exploration of the relationship between diet, particularly protein consumption, and cancer risk.
- Reflect on your own dietary choices and habits and assess how they might align with the research findings.
- Contemplate the impact of environment on health, including the potential role of environmental cues in shaping and maintaining healthier habits.

ACTIONABLE MOVEMENTS

1. Explore Dietary Changes: Consider adopting a diet that is lower in animal protein and higher in plant-based protein. The research highlighted in "The China Study" suggests that this dietary approach may help reduce the risk of cancer. Incorporating more fruits, vegetables, whole grains, and plant-based sources of protein can be beneficial.

2. Be Informed About Fungal Infections: Learn about the potential connection between fungal infections and diseases, including cancer. While not all diseases are directly linked to fungi, being aware of the risks and symptoms of fungal infections can help you take preventive measures and seek timely medical attention if needed.

3. Maintain a Healthy pH Balance: Given the emphasis on acidic environments and their potential relation to cancer growth, consider adopting lifestyle habits that promote a balanced pH level in your body. This includes eating alkaline-rich foods and staying hydrated.

4. Question Traditional Cancer Treatments: If you or a loved one is diagnosed with cancer, it's important to have open discussions with your medical team about the available treatment options. Ask about the potential benefits, risks, and side effects of treatments like chemotherapy, radiotherapy, and surgery. Don't hesitate to seek second opinions and explore alternative treatments if you feel they align better with your health goals.

5. Consider Holistic Approaches: Investigate complementary and holistic approaches to cancer treatment and prevention. While these approaches should never replace medically proven treatments, they might provide additional support to your overall well-being. Consult with healthcare professionals who are knowledgeable about both traditional and alternative therapies.

6. Emphasize Emotional Well-being: Recognize the importance of emotional well-being in your journey towards healing. Emotional stress and psychological factors can impact your immune system and overall health. Consider practices such as meditation, mindfulness, therapy, and support groups to help manage stress and emotions.

7. Stay Informed About Research: Stay updated on the latest research in the field of oncology, cancer treatment, and disease prevention. As science evolves, new insights and treatment strategies may emerge. Keeping yourself informed empowers you to make well-informed decisions regarding your health.

8. Engage in Preventive Measures: Take proactive steps to prevent fungal infections by maintaining good hygiene, especially in areas prone to moisture. For individuals undergoing treatments like radiotherapy and surgery, follow recommended hygiene practices to minimize the risk of opportunistic infections.

Remember that any decisions related to your health should be made in consultation with qualified medical professionals. The chapter provides valuable insights, but individual cases can vary greatly, and medical expertise is essential in making informed choices.

Record your reflections, insights, and observations on the concepts discussed earlier.

Use this space to brainstorm, sketch, or jot down any questions that arise in your mind. Make it a truly personal experience.

CHAPTER 7:
THE ROLE OF GENES IN DISEASE
ARE WE IN BONDAGE
TO DEFECTIVE GENES?

Summary

The chapter delves into the intricate relationship between genetics and disease, exploring the role of genes in causing diseases and the complex nature of genetic information. It starts by introducing the concept of genes and the human genome, which consists of three billion genetic letters forming the DNA code. The chapter explains that DNA is the blueprint for creating the structures and functions within the human body, containing instructions for everything from cellular energy production to organ development. Genes, the units of heredity, exist in pairs within 23 human chromosome pairs, with one gene from each parent.

The discovery of the DNA structure by Watson and Crick in 1953 is highlighted as a major breakthrough, leading to the understanding that DNA essentially holds the secret to life. This revelation gave rise to the belief that genes play a significant role in various aspects of human health and behavior. However, recent research has unveiled that environmental factors, encompassing nutrition, spirituality, emotions, and mental state, can profoundly influence gene expression. This insight has shifted the perspective on genetics as the sole determinant of health.

The chapter elaborates on how the environment impacts gene expression during prenatal development. It discusses how influences during pregnancy can affect genetic expression and shape an individual's health and abilities. Notably, emotional and social factors are cited as particularly influential in shaping the expression of genes in early childhood and beyond.

The concept of genes as a loaded gun and lifestyle as the trigger is introduced to underscore the interaction between genetics and environment in determining health outcomes. The author posits that merely 2 percent of diseases can be attributed solely to genes, highlighting that genetic predisposition alone is insufficient to cause diseases.

The discussion then shifts to factors that damage DNA, compromising cellular health. These include a drop in oxygen levels, environmental poisons like chemicals and heavy metals, alcohol, tobacco smoke, and even toxic emotions such as fear and anxiety. Such factors can lead to DNA mutations and subsequent health issues.

The chapter emphasizes the essential role of minerals and nutrients in maintaining DNA integrity. The structure and functioning of DNA strands are depicted as reliant on polysaccharides (complex carbohydrates), amino acids, and minerals like magnesium, selenium, potassium, and others. Deficiencies in these nutrients can lead to mutations and impaired cellular function. The text further explains that mineral deficiencies often arise due to impoverished soils, exposure to environmental toxins, dehydration, and poor dietary habits.

The positive news is presented in the form of the human body's inherent ability to heal itself when provided with optimal conditions, particularly appropriate nutrition. The significance of minerals in DNA structure is highlighted, with an emphasis on organic foods and plants rich in nutrients. The concept of "superfoods" is introduced, focusing on specific plants that offer exceptional healing properties due to their high mineral content. Stinging nettle, aloe vera, and comfrey are mentioned as examples, with their impressive mineral profiles and potential for aiding DNA repair and restoration.

The chapter concludes by discussing the potential of Orbitally Rearranged Monatomic Elements (ORMES), which are altered forms of minerals found in seawater. These ORMES have been studied for their ability to interact with human DNA and potentially repair damage. The chapter underscores the critical importance of minerals in maintaining DNA structure and the overall health of the body.

In essence, the chapter navigates through the intricate relationship between genetics and disease, highlighting the multifaceted interplay between genes and the environment. It emphasizes the role of minerals and nutrients in maintaining DNA integrity and promoting overall health, ultimately offering a nuanced perspective on the intricate web of factors contributing to human well-being.

LESSONS AND KEY POINTS FROM THIS CHAPTER

1. **Genes and Human Genome:** Genes are fundamental units of heredity found in the human genome, consisting of three billion genetic letters encoded in DNA. This genetic information guides the development and function of various structures and processes within the body.

2. **Role of DNA:** DNA is a complex molecule that holds the instructions for building and maintaining the human body. It contains the code for both small-scale functions, such as cellular energy production, and large-scale processes like organ formation.

3. **Genetic Pairs:** Genes exist in pairs within the 23 human chromosome pairs, with one gene inherited from each parent. These genes contain information that influences various characteristics, talents, and predispositions.

4. **Genetic Breakthrough:** Watson and Crick's discovery of the DNA structure in 1953 marked a significant scientific breakthrough, revealing the "secret of life" and establishing the idea that DNA rules the processes of life.

5. **Environmental Influence:** Recent research challenges the belief that genes are the primary determinants of health and behavior. Environmental factors such as nutrition, emotions, spirituality, and mental state have been found to significantly impact gene expression.

6. **Prenatal Influence:** The prenatal environment plays a crucial role in shaping genetic expression. Influences during pregnancy affect genetic development and have a lasting impact on an individual's physical and mental health.

7. **Genes and Lifestyle:** While genetics play a role in disease susceptibility, lifestyle factors have a profound impact on health outcomes. The metaphor "Genetics loads the gun, but lifestyle pulls the trigger" underscores the importance of healthy living.

8. **DNA Damage:** Factors such as low oxygen levels, environmental toxins, alcohol, tobacco smoke, and negative emotions can damage DNA, leading to mutations and potential health issues.

9. **Mineral Deficiencies:** Minerals and nutrients are essential for maintaining DNA integrity and cellular health. Deficiencies in minerals like magnesium, selenium, and potassium can lead to mutations and compromised cellular function.

10. **Organic Nutrition:** Providing the body with proper nutrition, particularly through organic foods rich in minerals, is vital for DNA repair and overall health.

11. **Superfoods:** Certain foods with exceptional mineral content, like stinging nettle, aloe vera, and comfrey, offer potential benefits for DNA repair and restoration.

12. **ORMES and DNA Repair:** Orbitally Rearranged Monatomic Elements (ORMES) are altered forms of minerals found in seawater. These elements are being studied for their potential to interact with human DNA and repair damage.

13. **Body's Self-Healing Ability:** The human body has an innate ability to heal itself under the right conditions, especially when provided with optimal nutrition and an environment that supports health.

14. **Minerals in the Genome:** Minerals like aluminum, cobalt, B12, sodium, and others are present in the human genome in significant quantities. They play crucial roles in DNA structure, cellular function, and overall health.

15. **Balancing Environment and Genetics:** The chapter underscores the delicate balance between genetics and the environment in determining health outcomes, highlighting the need for a comprehensive approach to well-being.

REFLECTION QUESTIONS

How does the interplay between genetics and environment influence your perception of health and disease?

In what ways have you witnessed the impact of lifestyle choices on your well-being, considering the concept that genetics loads the gun while lifestyle pulls the trigger?

Are there specific habits or behaviors you've adopted due to your environment that you would like to reconsider or modify for better health outcomes?

How can you create an environment that supports positive lifestyle changes, considering the importance of nutrients and minerals for DNA health?

Reflect on the concept of your body's self-healing ability. What steps can you take to enhance this ability through your environment and lifestyle choices?

MILESTONE GOALS

Understanding Genetic-Environmental Interaction: Gain a comprehensive understanding of how genes and the environment interact to influence health and disease. Explore the nuances of genetic expression and how factors like nutrition, emotions, and environmental toxins impact overall well-being.

Empowering Personal Health Choices: Use the insights from the chapter to empower oneself to make informed health choices. Learn to balance genetic predispositions with lifestyle changes and environmental factors to proactively improve and maintain health.

Implementing Practical Changes: Apply the knowledge gained to make practical changes in daily life. Identify and modify habits influenced by the environment, such as dietary choices and emotional well-being. Incorporate mineral-rich foods and superfoods into the diet to support DNA health, and create an environment that nurtures self-healing and overall well-being.

ACTIONABLE MOVEMENTS

1. Assess Your Environment: Take time to evaluate your living and working environments. Identify any potential sources of toxins or pollutants that could be affecting your health. Consider ways to reduce exposure to these harmful substances.

2. Prioritize Nutrient-Rich Foods: Make a conscious effort to include nutrient-dense foods in your diet. Incorporate dark green leafy vegetables, legumes, nuts, seeds, and foods rich in minerals like magnesium and selenium. Aim to replace processed and unhealthy options with whole, organic foods.

3. Mindful Emotions: Practice emotional awareness and management. Cultivate positive emotions such as love, joy, and peace, and work on managing negative emotions like stress and anxiety. Understand that emotional well-being can impact your genetic expression.

4. Create Supportive Cues: Modify your environment to encourage healthier habits. For instance, if you want to exercise more, place your workout gear somewhere visible as a reminder. Organize your kitchen to make healthy food choices more accessible and tempting.

5. Learn about ORMES: Research Orbitally Rearranged Monatomic Elements (ORMES) and their potential impact on DNA repair. Consult with professionals if you're interested in exploring supplements or natural sources of ORMES that could support your health goals.

6. Mindful Consumption: Be aware of the substances you're exposing yourself to, such as alcohol, tobacco, and processed foods. Make conscious choices to reduce or eliminate these harmful substances from your life.

7. Start with Small Changes: Begin by setting achievable goals. Choose one habit or aspect of your environment to focus on initially. For instance, commit to drinking more water, incorporating one superfood into your diet, or practicing daily emotional self-care.

8. Education and Research: Further your understanding of epigenetics and how environmental factors impact genetic expression. Stay informed about new research and findings in this field to refine your approach to maintaining health.

9. Monitor Progress: Keep track of your changes and their impact on your well-being. Regularly assess how your modified habits and environment are influencing your health. Adapt your approach as needed based on your observations.

Remember, these actionable movements are meant to be personalized to your specific circumstances and goals. Consult with healthcare professionals before making major changes, especially if you have pre-existing health conditions.

Record your reflections, insights, and observations on the concepts discussed earlier.

Use this space to brainstorm, sketch, or jot down any questions that arise in your mind. Make it a truly personal experience.

CHAPTER 8:
FUEL FOR LIFE
FOOD PERFORMS
OR DEFORMS

Summary

In this chapter, the author emphasizes the remarkable capacity of the human body to heal itself, provided it receives the appropriate conditions. Central to these conditions is the role of nutrition, echoing Hippocrates' famous adage, "Let food be your medicine, and medicine be your food." The chapter explores the profound impact of dietary choices on the body's ability to heal and thrive.

Nutritional Status and Cell Health: The chapter underscores that the human body is essentially a collection of cells, and the overall health of the body hinges on the nutritional status of each cell. Cells derive their nourishment from the food we consume. When food is grown in mineral-rich soil, it becomes rich in essential nutrients, including vitamins and minerals. Conversely, repetitive farming practices that deplete soil of its minerals result in impoverished plants and ultimately, malnourished individuals.

The Importance of Fiber: Fiber is highlighted as a critical component of nutrition, found abundantly in vegetables, whole grains, fruits, legumes, seeds, and nuts. Fiber plays a crucial role in stimulating peristalsis, the movement of food through the gastrointestinal tract, ensuring proper digestion and waste elimination. Additionally, fiber is closely tied to vitamins and minerals, making it essential for the body's biochemical reactions.

Protein for Cell Repair: Protein is labeled as an essential nutrient, vital for cell repair and DNA maintenance. Amino acids, the building blocks of proteins, are required for cellular repair processes. Without sufficient protein intake, the body's ability to heal is compromised. The chapter also delves into the significance of vegetarian sources of protein found in seeds, legumes, nuts, and grains.

The Role of Fats: Fats are explored as essential components of the cell membrane and as sources of energy. The chapter differentiates between "killer fats" and "healing fats." Killer fats are those laden with toxins, such as animal fats exposed to environmental contaminants, refined sugars, and carbohydrates that can lead to excessive glucose levels and fat storage, as well as heat-altered fats found in fried foods and margarine. In contrast, healing fats encompass polyunsaturated fats like omega-3 and omega-6, monounsaturated fats found in almonds and olives, and even saturated fats like coconut oil, which offer various health benefits.

Carbohydrates and Their Impact: The chapter highlights the excessive consumption of carbohydrates in modern diets, particularly in urban areas. High carbohydrate intake is linked to health issues, including diabetes and obesity. Moreover, the chapter discusses gluten sensitivity, attributing it to factors such as early introduction of grains to infants and the complex gluten structure in modern hybridized wheat varieties.

In conclusion, this chapter underscores the profound connection between nutrition and the body's ability to heal and maintain health. It emphasizes the importance of choosing foods rich in essential nutrients, fiber, proteins, and the right fats while being mindful of the potential pitfalls of modern dietary choices. The chapter advocates for a balanced and conscious approach to nutrition tailored to individual needs and circumstances.

LESSONS AND KEY POINTS FROM THIS CHAPTER

1. **The Body's Natural Healing Capacity:** The human body has a remarkable ability to heal itself when provided with the right conditions. These conditions primarily include proper nutrition.

2. **"Let Food Be Your Medicine":** The famous quote from Hippocrates, "Let food be your medicine, and medicine be your food," underscores the significance of nutrition in maintaining health and aiding the body's healing processes.

3. **Cellular Health:** The body is composed of cells, and the nutritional status of each cell plays a pivotal role in determining overall health. The food we consume directly impacts the health of our cells.

4. **Mineral-Rich Soil:** Food grown in mineral-rich soil is essential for providing the necessary vitamins and minerals that cells need to function optimally. Depleted soils result in impoverished plants and, eventually, malnourished individuals.

5. **Fiber's Importance:** Fiber, primarily found in vegetables, whole grains, fruits, legumes, seeds, and nuts, is crucial for maintaining digestive health. It stimulates peristalsis and is closely tied to vitamins and minerals.

6. **Protein for Cell Repair:** Protein is essential for cell repair and DNA maintenance. Amino acids, the building blocks of proteins, are required for cellular repair processes. A diet lacking in protein can hinder the body's ability to heal.

7. **Distinguishing "Killer" and "Healing" Fats:** Fats in the diet are not all the same. "Killer" fats, laden with toxins, can be harmful, while "healing" fats like polyunsaturated fats (omega-3 and omega-6), monounsaturated fats, and specific saturated fats like coconut oil offer health benefits.

8. **Excessive Carbohydrate Consumption:** Modern diets, especially in urban areas, often include excessive carbohydrate intake. This can lead to health issues, including diabetes and obesity.

9. **Gluten Sensitivity:** A significant portion of the population may be sensitive to gluten, primarily found in wheat and oats. Factors like early introduction of grains to infants and the complex gluten structure in modern hybridized wheat varieties can contribute to this sensitivity.

10. **Individualized Nutrition:** Nutrition should be tailored to individual needs, taking into account factors such as size, height, weight, age, fitness, physical and mental activity, and overall health. A balanced approach to nutrition is essential for promoting well-being and healing.

REFLECTION QUESTIONS

Are you mindful of the nutritional quality of the foods you consume on a daily basis? How can you improve your diet to better support your overall health and well-being?

_____

_____

_____

Do you pay attention to the source of the food you eat, considering factors like soil quality and farming practices? How can you make more informed choices about the origins of your food?

What role does fiber play in your diet, and do you ensure you get enough of it? How might increasing your fiber intake benefit your digestive health and overall vitality?

Are you aware of the types of fats you consume regularly? Can you identify "killer" fats from "healing" fats in your diet, and how might adjusting your fat intake positively impact your health?

Considering the prevalence of high-carbohydrate diets in urban settings, how does your own carbohydrate consumption align with your health goals? Are there adjustments you can make to your carbohydrate intake to support your well-being?

MILESTONE GOALS

Optimize Nutritional Choices: Your first goal can be to make more conscious and informed choices about the foods you consume. Aim to prioritize foods that are grown in mineral-rich soil, ensuring they provide essential vitamins and minerals. This goal involves seeking out high-quality, organic, or locally sourced produce whenever possible.

Balanced Nutrient Intake: Set a goal to achieve a balanced intake of essential nutrients. This includes ensuring you get an adequate amount of fiber, protein, and healthy fats in your daily diet. You can plan meals that incorporate a variety of foods rich in these nutrients, such as vegetables, legumes, seeds, nuts, and lean protein sources.

Mindful Carbohydrate Consumption: Given the prevalence of high-carbohydrate diets in urban settings, aim to be mindful of your carbohydrate consumption. Strive to reduce your intake of refined carbohydrates, sugars, and gluten-containing foods if you suspect sensitivity. Opt for complex carbohydrates like whole grains, and adapt your carbohydrate intake to suit your individual needs, activity levels, and health goals.

ACTIONABLE MOVEMENTS

1. Assess Your Current Diet: Begin by evaluating your current dietary habits. Keep a food journal for a week to track what you typically eat. Take note of the types of foods, their sources, and your portion sizes.

2. Prioritize Nutrient-Rich Foods: Make a conscious effort to prioritize nutrient-rich foods in your diet. This includes incorporating more vegetables, whole grains, legumes, seeds, nuts, and lean proteins into your meals.

3. Source Quality Food: Whenever possible, choose foods that are grown in mineral-rich soil and sourced from reputable suppliers. Consider buying organic or locally grown produce to ensure higher nutritional value.

4. Increase Fiber Intake: Focus on increasing your daily fiber intake. Aim to incorporate a variety of fiber-rich foods into your meals, such as whole grains, vegetables, fruits, and legumes. Gradually increase fiber to avoid digestive discomfort.

5. Choose Healthy Fats: Be selective about the fats you consume. Opt for sources of healthy fats, such as avocados, olive oil, nuts, and seeds. Reduce your intake of trans fats and processed fats found in fried and packaged foods.

6. Balance Protein Intake: Ensure you're getting enough protein in your diet, especially if you're on a vegetarian or plant-based diet. Explore various protein sources like beans, lentils, tofu, and lean meats if you're not vegetarian.

7. Mindful Carbohydrate Consumption: Evaluate your carbohydrate intake and consider adjusting it to align with your health goals. Reduce consumption of refined carbohydrates and sugary foods, opting for whole grains and gluten-free options if necessary.

8. Meal Planning: Plan your meals in advance to ensure you're incorporating a variety of nutrient-rich foods. Create weekly meal plans and shopping lists to facilitate healthier choices.

Remember that making dietary changes may require gradual adjustments, and it's important to prioritize sustainability in your choices. By taking these actionable steps, you can work towards a healthier and more balanced diet that supports your overall well-being.

Record your reflections, insights, and observations on the concepts discussed earlier.

Use this space to brainstorm, sketch, or jot down any questions that arise in your mind. Make it a truly personal experience.

CHAPTER 9:
CONQUERING CANDIDA
AND OTHER FUNGUS/YEAST
RELATED PROBLEMSOO

Summary

In this chapter, the focus is on conquering fungal and yeast-related problems within the body. The chapter begins by acknowledging the diverse ways in which fungus can enter the body and the wide range of symptoms it can cause. It emphasizes that the following program is a foundational approach, with the understanding that each individual will need to fine-tune it based on factors such as age, fitness level, environment, health status, and the severity of their condition. The ultimate goal is to design a personalized self-healing program.

The chapter outlines a three-pronged approach to combat candida, fungus, and yeast outbreaks:

1. STARVE THE FUNGUS

The first step involves starving the fungus by eliminating its primary sources of sustenance:

<u>Sugars:</u> All forms of sugar, especially cane and beet sugar, must be removed from the diet. This includes honey, sweeteners, fruits, and fruit juices. Exceptions are made for Granny Smith apples and grapefruit, which have lower sugar content and contain antifungal properties.

<u>Yeast:</u> All yeast-containing foods and beverages should be eliminated, including yeast bread (except sourdough), alcoholic beverages, yeast spreads, yeast extracts, brewer's yeast,

mushrooms, and soy sauce.

Old Food: Any cooked food over two days old or with traces of mold should be discarded. Rice, in particular, is susceptible to fungal growth and should be consumed freshly cooked.

Corn and Wheat: These grains are vulnerable to fungal growth during storage and should be eliminated during the initial stages of overcoming a fungal problem.

Peanuts: Peanuts are notorious for fungal infestation and should be avoided, especially in the form of peanut butter.

Meat: Meat from animals fed moldy grains can contain fungal contaminants. Additionally, casein in meat and dairy products may encourage fungal growth. Aged cheeses and most dairy products can also show fungal infestation.

Environment: Ensure there are no damp, dark areas in your home where mold can thrive. Be cautious of compost bins and mulch during their fungal breakdown stages.

Chemicals: Eliminate contact with chemicals found in cleaning products, shampoos, conditioners, soap, laundry detergents, and nylon clothing.

Heavy Metals: Be cautious of mercury and dioxin contamination in fish, especially larger fish. Amalgam dental fillings can contain up to 60% mercury and are recommended for replacement with mercury-free white fillings.

2. KILL THE FUNGUS

The chapter also discusses various herbs and foods that can help control fungus, yeast, and candida:

Herbs: Garlic, olive leaf extract, oregano oil, Pau D'Arco, horopito, and grapefruit seed extract are all highlighted for their antifungal properties.

Iodine: Lugol's solution, containing iodine and potassium iodide, is recommended for its strong fungicidal effects.

Alkalize: Creating an alkaline environment in the body is another strategy to combat fungus, as it thrives in an acidic environment.

Food: Certain foods, like coconut, legumes, raw nuts, and seeds, contain antifungal properties and can be incorporated into the diet. It's suggested to alternate herbal medicines every two weeks to maintain their effectiveness.

3. RESTORE THE BALANCE

The chapter acknowledges that an imbalance in gut flora is often a contributing factor in fungal problems. The gastrointestinal tract houses a large number of microorganisms, including beneficial yeasts and bacteria. However, factors like drugs, antibiotics, alcohol, refined sugar, stress, and unhealthy lifestyles can disrupt this balance, allowing opportunistic organisms like Candida to multiply. To restore balance, the chapter recommends:

Encouraging the presence of acidophilus and bifidus: These healthy bacteria can be reintroduced through cultured foods like sourdough bread, sauerkraut, miso, tofu, tempeh, soy yogurt, and probiotic supplements.

Next, the chapter introduces the "ANTIFUNGAL FOOD PROGRAM," which emphasizes the significant impact of diet on the body's environment. It suggests adhering to stage one of the program for at least one month and then implementing stage two based on the severity of the condition. This approach aims to not only combat existing fungal issues but also maintain long-term health and balance.

Below is an example of a menu that adheres to the stage one food lists on the following page:

Example of a Daily Stage One Menu

BREAKFAST	LUNCH	DINNER
▶ Grapefruit or granny smith apple	▶ Raw salad with a salad dressing (see recipes on page 75)	▶ Bowl of *Split Pea Soup* (page 75)
▶ Cooked grain (such as millet, rice, quinoa or buckwheat)	WITH	AND/OR
ADD	▶ Baked potato/sweet potato and steamed carrots and broccoli	▶ A few Ryvita crackers with avocado and tomato
▶ Savoury lentils	WITH	
OR	▶ *Chickpea Cardamom Casserole* (page 75)	
▶ Stewed apples topped with coconut cream or soy yoghurt	PLUS	
	▶ 8 pecan nuts	

The Antifungal Diet - Stage One

	STAGE 1 FOODS INCLUDED	STAGE 1 FOODS EXCLUDED
SUGARS	None	Honey, maple syrup, artificial and herbal sweeteners, and all other sugars
FRUIT	Granny Smith apples, grapefruit, lemons, avocado and tomato	All other fruit, including their juices
VEGETABLES	Fresh, unblemished vegetables and their juices	
BEVERAGES	Herb teas, water and unsweetened soymilk	Tea, coffee, fruit juice, cola and soft drinks
GRAINS	Freshly cooked brown rice, spelt, sourdough bread, quinoa, amaranth, millet, buckwheat, rye and a small amount of non-wheat or corn pasta	Wheat and corn
LEGUMES	All legumes including soy and soy products	Peanuts
YEAST PRODUCTS	None	Yeasted bread, mushrooms, alcohol and marmite/vegemite
VINEGAR	Black olives in brine permitted	Pickles, salad dressings, soy sauce and green olives
OILS	Extra Virgin olive oil, flaxseed oil and coconut oil	Margarine, corn and peanut oil
NUTS	All raw nuts, including coconut	Peanuts and pistachios
SEEDS	All seeds such as pumpkin, sesame and sunflower	
CULTURED FOODS	Tofu, soy yoghurt, miso, sauerkraut and tempeh	All aged cheeses

The Antifungal Diet - Stage Two

Stage two of the Antifungal Diet is a continuation of stage one with some additional modifications:

Fruits: In this stage, all berries are added to the fruit section, expanding the options for individuals following the diet. Furthermore, maple syrup and stevia are introduced as sweeteners.

The Cancer-Conquering Diet

This diet is designed to empower the body to combat cancer naturally. It underscores the body's inherent ability to heal itself when provided with the right conditions. The key premise of this diet is that cancer cells self-destruct when deprived of glucose, their preferred energy source. Due to their rapid metabolism, cancer cells are more susceptible to glucose deprivation.

Important considerations regarding cancer and nutrition:

Malnutrition: The primary cause of cancer is malnutrition at the cellular level. A well-nourished body is less prone to cancer.

Toxins: Exposure to chemicals, poisons, heavy metals, excessive hormones, and fungus may not lead to cancer if the body has adequate nutrients to detoxify and a strong immune system.

The recommended food program is intended for a six-week period, during which it drastically reduces the intake of glucose to hinder the growth of cancer cells. The goal is to minimize glucose levels as much as possible, as cancer cells thrive on sugar. This dietary plan provides plant protein, essential vitamins and minerals, essential fatty acids, and sufficient carbohydrates to support the body's healing response and meet all nutritional requirements for optimal health.

Foods in the Cancer-Conquering Diet

Legumes: This category includes lentils, chickpeas, red kidney beans, and soybeans. Thoroughly rinsing and cooking them until soft is essential. Discarding the cooking water and adding flavorings are also recommended. Culinary herbs can aid in the digestion of legumes. This section also includes tofu, soy yogurt, and miso.

Vegetables: A wide range of vegetables is encouraged, including asparagus, peas, beans, cooked tomatoes (rich in lycopene with antifungal properties), onions, garlic, ginger, root vegetables (potatoes, sweet potatoes, pumpkin, beetroot, parsnips, carrots, turnips), green leafy vegetables (high in anticancer properties, such as celery, basil, coriander, oregano, rosemary, and parsley), and brassica vegetables (cabbage, kale, turnip, brussels sprouts, broccoli, and cauliflower, lightly steamed to avoid inhibiting thyroid function).

Grains: Brown rice is recommended as an antifungal option when cooked fresh and consumed promptly. Other grains such as millet, buckwheat, and quinoa can also be included.

<u>Fruit:</u> Avocado, lemon, lime, and tomato are the suggested fruits.

<u>Oils:</u> Olive oil, coconut oil, flax oil, and coconut cream are the approved oils.

<u>Fresh nuts and seeds:</u> All raw nuts (including coconut) and seeds like pumpkin, sesame, and sunflower are permissible.

Additions:

<u>Cayenne pepper</u>
<u>Turmeric:</u> Known for its high antifungal properties.
<u>Celtic salt:</u> Approximately 1–1 ½ teaspoons per day.

Supplements:

<u>Vitamin C:</u> ½ teaspoon, three times daily, with 1 teaspoon of Aloe vera (antifungal).
<u>Vitamin B Complex:</u> 1 teaspoon, two times daily (kick-starts normal metabolic function and reduces toxicity of fungi).
<u>Acidophilus/Bifidus:</u> ½ teaspoon daily to aid nutrient absorption (antifungal).
<u>Mineral supplement:</u> 1 teaspoon, twice daily.
<u>Bitter herbs:</u> Gentian, dandelion, golden seal, licorice, and ginger to aid digestion.
<u>Antifungal herbs:</u> These should be alternated every fortnight. A list of these herbs is provided in the section 'Conquering Candida.'
<u>Four green drinks daily:</u> Consumed between meals to support overall health and well-being. This diet is a powerful tool to create an environment within the body that discourages cancer cell growth while promoting overall health and vitality.

Example of a Cancer-Conquering Diet

BREAKFAST	Lunch	DINNER
▶ Salad, such as tomato, cucumber, avocado	▶ Salad such as grated carrot/ beetroot, celery, lettuce, olives, avocado, with *Tahini mayo* dressing (page 79)	▶ *The Mighty Minestrone Soup* (page 79) or herb tea.
PLUS	▶ Baked potato and pumpkin or sweet potato	
▶ ½ cup freshly cooked brown rice	▶ Stir-fry vegetables	
▶ 1 cup *Quick Brown Lentils* (page 79)	▶ *Lovely Lima Beans* (page 79)	
▶ Steamed vegetables	▶ 6 macadamia nuts	
▶ 8-10 almonds		

Transition After the Cancer-Conquering Diet

After completing the six-week Cancer-Conquering Diet, it is advisable to transition to the following stages:

<u>Stage One of the Antifungal Program:</u> Continue with stage one for at least two months.

<u>Stage Two of the Antifungal Program (Maintenance Program):</u> Following stage one, move on to stage two, which serves as a maintenance program.

A Comment on Soy

Soybeans have been a dietary staple in Asia for millennia, consumed in various forms such as fresh, dried legumes, tofu, or soybean milk. Asian populations are renowned for their long, healthy lives, partially attributed to soybean consumption, along with their emphasis on fresh vegetables, clean water, and active lifestyles that are notably low in caffeine, alcohol, and sugar. It's important to note that traditionally, soybeans in Asia are non-genetically modified and organically grown, with the entire soybean being utilized.

Dr. Harry Miller, an English surgeon who worked extensively in China during the early 1800s, played a pioneering role in promoting soybean milk, which saved the lives of numerous Chinese infants. However, in recent years, there has been considerable media coverage raising concerns about soy consumption, particularly its alleged associations with hormonal cancers like breast cancer, uterine cancer, and prostate cancer. Interestingly, there appears to be a stark contrast between soybean consumption in Asia and developed countries.

The soybean itself is recognized as one of the most potent anticancer plants on Earth, boasting twice the protein content of most other legumes and containing high-quality plant oils. Thus, it is argued that the issue lies not with the soybean itself but rather in how it is cultivated and processed.

Genetically modified soybeans, introduced in the United States in 1996, have become prevalent in leading soybean-producing countries worldwide. Consumption of genetically modified soybeans, especially when not organically grown and refined into isolated forms for food, has been linked to various health concerns, including allergies. Fortunately, Australia mandates the labeling of genetically modified foods, and while genetically modified soybeans are not grown in Australia, they can be found as ingredients in various imported food products like chocolate, potato chips, margarine, mayonnaise, biscuits, and bread.

Given the aforementioned concerns, it is essential to ensure that the soy products you purchase are made from non-genetically modified, organically grown soybeans, utilizing the whole bean. One convenient way to incorporate soy into your diet is through tofu, a highly digestible and protein-rich option. Keep in mind that tofu is a neutral base and can be transformed into a delicious culinary delight with the addition of appropriate flavorings.

LESSONS AND KEY POINTS FROM THIS CHAPTER

1. Fungal and Yeast-Related Problems: The chapter addresses the prevalence and impact of fungal and yeast-related problems in the body, emphasizing the diverse ways these issues can enter the body and manifest through various symptoms.

2. Personalized Self-Healing: It underscores the importance of designing a personalized self-healing program based on individual factors such as age, fitness, environment, health status, and the severity of the condition.

3. Three-Pronged Approach: The chapter introduces a comprehensive three-pronged approach to combat candida, fungus, and yeast outbreaks in the body: starving the fungus, killing the fungus, and restoring the balance of beneficial microbes.

4. Starving the Fungus: Key elements of this approach involve eliminating sugars and yeast from the diet, being cautious of old or moldy food, avoiding corn and wheat, peanuts, and being mindful of meat sources. Additionally, maintaining a mold-free environment and reducing exposure to chemicals and heavy metals are essential.

5. Killing the Fungus: The chapter highlights various herbs and foods with antifungal properties, including garlic, olive leaf extract, oregano oil, Pau D'Arco, horopito, grapefruit seed extract, and iodine. Alkalizing the body is also recommended.

6. Restore the Balance: A significant contributing factor to fungal problems is an imbalance in gut flora. The chapter stresses the importance of encouraging the presence of healthy bacteria like acidophilus and bifidus through cultured foods and probiotic supplements.

7. The Antifungal Food Program: This program focuses on the impact of diet on the body's environment. It recommends adhering to stage one for at least one month, followed by stage two for long-term maintenance, with adjustments based on the severity of the condition.

8. Transition After the Cancer-Conquering Diet: Following the Cancer-Conquering Diet, individuals are advised to transition to the antifungal program's stages for long-term health maintenance.

9. Soybean Considerations: The chapter addresses the controversy surrounding soy consumption, highlighting the historical health benefits associated with traditional Asian soybean consumption. It emphasizes the importance of choosing non-genetically

modified, organically grown soybeans and utilizing the whole bean for maximum health benefits.

10. Soy as a Nutrient-Rich Food: Soybeans are recognized for their high protein content, essential fatty acids, and potent anticancer properties when consumed in their natural, unprocessed form.

REFLECTION QUESTIONS

Are you aware of any dietary habits or food choices that might be contributing to fungal or yeast-related health issues in your body?

How willing are you to make significant dietary changes to address potential fungal or yeast-related problems in your health?

What is your understanding of the impact of diet on your overall health and well-being, particularly in relation to preventing or managing chronic diseases like cancer?

Have you ever considered the quality and source of soy products in your diet? Are you open to making informed choices when it comes to soy consumption?

In your pursuit of optimal health, how do you plan to incorporate the principles of starving, killing, and balancing in your approach to managing health-related challenges?

MILESTONE GOALS

Implement a Healthier Diet: Your first goal could be to revamp your diet by reducing or eliminating foods that are known to feed fungal and yeast-related issues in the body, such as sugars, yeast-containing foods, and mold-prone items. You can aim to start the process of "starving the fungus" by adopting a more antifungal diet.

Explore Antifungal Herbs and Foods: Another goal could be to explore and incorporate antifungal herbs and foods into your daily meals. You might want to experiment with garlic, olive leaf extract, oregano oil, and other recommended items to see how they impact your health.

Increase Awareness of Soy Choices: If you consume soy products, your goal could be to become more informed about the quality and source of these products. You can strive to make conscious choices, opting for non-genetically modified, organically grown soybeans, and embracing soy as a nutrient-rich food in its natural form.

ACTIONABLE MOVEMENTS

1. Audit Your Diet:

- Start by thoroughly examining your current diet. Identify foods that are high in sugar, yeast, or potential mold contamination. Take note of any processed foods that might contain hidden sugars.

2. Sugar Reduction:

- Begin the process of reducing sugar consumption. Gradually eliminate sources of added sugars like sugary snacks, sodas, and desserts. Focus on consuming whole fruits with lower sugar content like Granny Smith apples and grapefruit.

3. Yeast-Free Diet:

- Cut out yeast-containing foods and beverages from your diet, such as yeast bread, alcoholic drinks, and yeast extracts. Replace these items with alternatives that are yeast-free.

4. Fresh and Organic:

- Prioritize fresh, organic, and non-genetically modified foods in your diet. When possible, opt for organically grown produce to minimize exposure to pesticides and herbicides.

5. Incorporate Antifungal Foods:

- Introduce antifungal foods into your meals, such as garlic, olive leaf extract, oregano oil, Pau D'Arco, and grapefruit seed extract. Experiment with these ingredients to create flavorful and healthful dishes.

6. Check Soy Sources:

- If you consume soy products, check product labels for information about the source of soybeans. Aim to purchase products made from non-genetically modified, organically grown soybeans. Choose whole soybean products like tofu for maximum health benefits.

7. Gut Health:

- Invest in your gut health by incorporating probiotic-rich foods and supplements. Explore cultured foods like sauerkraut, miso, and soy yogurt. Consider taking acidophilus and bifidus supplements to support healthy gut flora.

8. Environmental Check:

- Evaluate your living environment for any signs of mold or dampness. Address any issues promptly to create a mold-free living space.

Remember that making gradual and sustainable changes to your diet and lifestyle can lead to long-term improvements in your health and well-being.

Record your reflections, insights, and observations on the concepts discussed earlier.

Use this space to brainstorm, sketch, or jot down any questions that arise in your mind. Make it a truly personal experience.

CHAPTER 10:
ACID AND ALKALINE BALANCE
PRECISION IS EVERYTHING

Summary

Fungus's relationship to acidity and alkalinity is crucial to understanding its impact on the human body. This connection is expressed through the pH scale, which measures the acidity or alkalinity of a substance. pH stands for "potential hydrogen," representing the concentration of hydrogen ions in a solution. Acidic substances release hydrogen ions when dissociated in water, while alkaline substances release hydroxyl ions. Neutral pH signifies an equilibrium between hydrogen and hydroxyl ions, indicating neither acidity nor alkalinity.

The pH balance, like a thermometer for body fluids, plays a vital role in regulating cellular processes. It influences enzymatic activity and the speed of electrical signals within the body. An acidic pH corresponds to a hot and fast environment, while an alkaline pH is associated with a slow and cool one. Maintaining the body's pH balance is crucial, as even slight deviations from the norm can signal potentially serious imbalances.

Blood pH, constantly monitored by the lungs and kidneys, is particularly significant. A blood pH of 7.22 can lead to a coma and death due to acidosis, while a pH of 8 can cause a coma and potential death from alkalosis. Although blood pH remains stable, cellular pH can change, and this can be assessed using litmus paper in urine and saliva. Severe and persistent acidity can force the body to draw calcium phosphates from bones, potentially resulting in conditions like osteoporosis.

When harmful microorganisms like bacteria, yeasts, and fungi are active in the body due to cell damage or infiltration, they create an acidic environment. These microorganisms thrive in such conditions, multiplying rapidly. Maintaining the correct pH in the body is essential for preventing the proliferation of these harmful organisms and is integral to addressing issues like fungus and cancer. Sodium bicarbonate, highly alkaline, has been successful in countering this acidic environment.

Green vegetables and grasses are rich sources of alkaline salts that combat fungal growth. Chlorophyll, the green pigment in plants, closely resembles human blood molecules and has therapeutic benefits, including antioxidant properties, virus and bacteria growth inhibition, cell repair stimulation, and detoxification. Incorporating green foods, such as salads or green supplements like barley or wheatgrass juice, can be a potent strategy for alkalizing and cleansing the body's tissues.

The food we consume affects our body's pH balance. The mitochondria, found in cells, burn glucose from food to produce energy, leaving an acidic or alkaline ash residue based on the food's mineral composition. Alkaline-forming elements include calcium, potassium, magnesium, sodium, and iron, while sulfur, phosphorus, chlorine, and iodine are acid-forming elements. A chart categorizes various foods from most acid-forming to most alkaline-forming.

However, there are exceptions, such as fruit. In a body with a yeast/fungus issue, fruit consumption can lead to the production of lactic acid, acetic acid, uric acid, and alcohol by the fungus, creating an environment conducive to fungal growth. Nightshade vegetables like tomatoes, eggplant, capsicum, and potatoes can exacerbate inflammation in the presence of an inflammatory condition but tend to have an alkaline effect when inflammation is absent.

To maintain a balanced pH, it's recommended that 80% of one's food intake consists of alkaline-forming foods and 20% of acid-forming foods. Eliminating cane and beet sugar, alcohol, caffeine, tobacco, and reducing meat and dairy consumption while increasing vegetable intake can help maintain a pH balance of approximately 6.5 in the cells. Slightly acidic conditions are necessary for maintaining optimal electrical conductivity within cells.

Understanding the impact of certain dietary and lifestyle habits on the body's acid-alkaline balance is essential for maintaining overall health. Here, we delve deeper into the exceptions and lifestyle habits that influence this balance, as well as recommendations for achieving optimal pH levels.

Fruit and Fungal Interaction: The relationship between fruit consumption and the presence of yeast and fungus in the body is intriguing. Fungus thrives on sugar, especially refined cane sugar, but it can also utilize the glucose found in fruit. When consumed in a body with fungal issues, fruit sugars are rapidly consumed by the fungus, resulting in the production of lactic acid, acetic acid, uric acid, and alcohol. These acidic byproducts create an environment conducive to the rapid multiplication of fungi. However, in a fungus-free body, fruit can have an alkalizing and cleansing effect.

Nightshade Vegetables: Nightshade vegetables like tomatoes, eggplant, capsicum, and potatoes can influence inflammation. When inflammation is present, these vegetables tend to exacerbate it. An exception is when tomatoes are cooked without the skin; this process releases a powerful antioxidant called lycopene, which can inhibit inflammation, particularly in the prostate gland. In non-inflammatory conditions, nightshade vegetables, especially tomatoes, have a more alkaline effect. Personal adjustments may be necessary depending on individual health status.

Recommendations: To maintain an ideal pH balance in the body, it's advisable to structure your food program with 80 percent alkaline-forming foods and 20 percent acid-forming foods. This ratio helps maintain a cellular pH balance of around 6.5, which is slightly acidic, necessary for optimal electrical conductivity within cells. To achieve this balance, it's crucial to eliminate cane and beet sugar in all forms, abstain from alcohol, avoid all caffeine-containing drinks and foods, and steer clear of tobacco. Ideally, reduce or eliminate meat and dairy products while increasing your consumption of vegetables and other alkaline-forming foods.

Lifestyle Habits and Their Impact on pH Balance:

Habit 1: Oxygen: Adequate oxygen is vital for the body's well-being. Oxygen is essential for life and plays a crucial role in alkalizing the body. It invigorates and electrifies the body, soothing the nerves. Oxygen is particularly crucial for aerobic cells, as a deficiency forces cells to rely on anaerobic fermentation for energy. Fungal and cancer cells, both anaerobic, struggle to thrive in the presence of oxygen. Proper breathing habits, good posture, exercise, and exposure to fresh air can enhance oxygen intake.

Habit 2: Sunshine: Sunlight plays a vital role in alkalizing the body. It helps convert cholesterol under the skin into vitamin D, an essential nutrient for inhibiting cancer cell growth and aiding calcium metabolism. While too much or too little sun exposure can create acidity, approximately one hour of sunshine daily can help maintain an alkaline balance.

Habit 3: Temperance: Temperance involves avoiding substances that harm the body and consuming all good things in moderation. Alcohol, caffeine, refined sugar, tobacco, drugs, chemicals, and heavy metals can all induce acidity in the body. Eliminating these from your diet is crucial for maintaining the correct pH balance.

- Alcohol is a neurotoxin that inhibits the body's healing abilities and fosters an acidic environment, favorable for fungal growth.
- Caffeine is highly addictive and disrupts brain chemistry, leading to an acidic condition.

- Sugar is extremely acidic, promoting fungal growth and an environment that fungus thrives in.
- Tobacco inhibits oxygen availability in cells, creating an invitation for fungal development.
- Drugs and chemicals can also induce acidity, so reducing contact with them is advisable.

Habit 4: Rest: Adequate sleep is essential for maintaining an alkaline state. The hours between 9 pm and 2 am are particularly significant, as the pineal gland releases hormones during this time that contribute to mood, learning capacity, pain relief, and overall rejuvenation. Early nights and a balanced sleep schedule can help achieve this alkalizing effect. Additionally, proper meal timing and spacing, combined with good posture and regular exercise, support the body's need for rest and digestion.

Incorporating these lifestyle habits and dietary recommendations can contribute to a balanced pH level in the body, promoting overall health and well-being. Achieving an ideal pH balance supports the body's ability to resist fungal growth and maintain optimal cellular function.

Habit 5: Exercise: The role of exercise in maintaining a balanced pH and overall health is significant. Just as too little exercise can lead to stagnation and acidity in the body, excessive exercise can also create an acidic environment. Exercise, especially aerobic activities that elevate the heart rate and respiration, helps increase oxygen availability to every cell in the body. Oxygen plays a pivotal role in alkalizing the body, and this is crucial because cancer cells struggle to survive in oxygen-rich environments.

In today's fast-paced world, sedentary lifestyles are becoming increasingly common due to the convenience of various time-saving devices. As a result, many individuals aren't moving their bodies enough to receive adequate oxygen. The body operates on a delicate balance, requiring both brain and body activities to be in equilibrium. Physical activity is essential for self-healing and preserving health. Aerobic exercise, which includes at least 20 minutes of increased heart rate and respiration, triggers the release of the human growth hormone (HGH).

HGH is a hormone with several benefits, including:

- Increasing the body's ability to utilize protein.
- Shifting the body from burning glucose to burning fat as fuel.
- Releasing an enzyme in cells that prompts the release of adipose fat stores.
- Enhancing blood circulation to the skin.

Athletes often rely on HGH for its performance-enhancing effects. This hormone's release during exercise contributes to its healing properties. A significant aspect of this effect is its alkalizing impact. Half an hour of daily exercise keeps the body in good working order, while one hour can even reverse major health problems like fungal issues and cancer. This exercise can be split into two 30-minute sessions or one 30-minute session plus two 15-minute sessions. Walking, swimming, and gardening are highly recommended exercises because they engage all major muscle groups. Exercise not only strengthens the heart, lungs, bones, and muscles but also tones and strengthens internal organs, ensuring optimal circulation, which is vital for perfect health.

Habit 6: Water: Water is often referred to as the "blue arteries of the earth" and has a significant alkalizing effect on the body. Many people experience acidity due to dehydration, as the average-sized human body loses about two to three liters of water daily. Unlike vehicles with reserve tanks, our bodies only receive the water we consume. To maintain proper hydration, it's essential to drink two to three liters of pure water daily, and more may be needed on very hot or active days. Water should be consumed between meals, with a pause half an hour before eating and a two-hour gap after meals to allow for optimal digestion.

It's important to note that drinking water with meals can dilute hydrochloric acid, necessary for digesting protein. The body best accepts water when consumed gradually throughout the day. When increasing water intake, ensuring sufficient salt intake is also crucial. Celtic salt, containing three types of magnesium, can help increase the delivery of water into the cells.

Habit 7: Salt: Sodium is the third most vital element for life, and it should be consumed in a balanced form, as found in nature. Sea water contains the highest concentration of sodium, along with 92 minerals. Celtic and Himalayan salts, unrefined sea salts, contain approximately 82 minerals. In contrast, table salt, commonly found on supermarket shelves, contains only sodium and chloride, creating an imbalanced, harsh, and dangerous salt. Injecting sodium chloride directly into the body could lead to fatality.

The human body requires sodium in its natural, balanced form, accompanied by various minerals. When consumed in this way, sodium has an alkalizing effect, ensuring a proper mineral balance in the body. Our tears, blood, urine, and even the amniotic fluid in which a baby swims in utero are all salty. Refined salt, with only sodium and chloride, contributes to an acidic condition in the body.

Habit 8: Mental Health: Maintaining positive mental health is the final piece of the alkalizing puzzle. Laughter, as Mark Twain noted, is a powerful force, and science has confirmed its ability to release healing hormones. The combination of the previous lifestyle habits creates a strong and nutritionally stable physical body, which provides the foundation for managing stress effectively.

A positive attitude, a merry heart, and trust in a higher power can significantly contribute to inner peace. The Bible emphasizes the importance of a peaceful mind and its alkalizing effect. Negative emotions such as grief, anxiety, discontent, remorse, guilt, resentment, and distrust can lead to physical deterioration and disease. On the other hand, faith, hope, and a positive outlook can facilitate healing. Faith, often accompanied by hope, is an alkaline emotion, while fear and its associated emotions are acidic.

Emotions have a tangible impact on our physical well-being, with fear and negativity exacerbating health issues and faith and positivity promoting healing. Science has revealed the brain's ability to rewire itself, indicating that even the most negative individuals can develop a positive outlook through diligence and exposure to positive influences.

Maintaining a positive mindset, free from negative influences, is crucial. Just as good nutrition strengthens the body, positive mental health supports the alkaline state of the mind. Maintaining hope, faith, and trust in a higher power can contribute to inner peace and overall alkalinity.

LESSONS AND KEY POINTS FROM THIS CHAPTER

Lesson 1: The Importance of pH Balance
- Maintaining the body's pH balance is essential for overall health and well-being.
- An acidic pH can lead to various health problems, while an alkaline pH is generally conducive to good health.

Lesson 2: The Impact of Diet on pH
- Diet plays a significant role in determining the body's pH balance.
- Consuming too many acidic-forming foods, such as sugar and processed foods, can lead to an acidic internal environment.

Lesson 3: Alkaline-Forming Foods
- A diet rich in alkaline-forming foods, including fruits and vegetables, helps maintain a healthy pH balance.
- These foods can have a cleansing and detoxifying effect on the body.

Lesson 4: Acidic-Forming Foods
- Acidic-forming foods, like sugar, caffeine, and processed foods, can contribute to an acidic internal environment.
- Excessive consumption of these foods should be avoided to maintain pH balance.

Lesson 5: Exceptions to Alkaline-Forming Foods
- Some fruits, like those with high sugar content, can temporarily contribute to acidity when consumed in excess.

Lesson 6: Nightshade Vegetables
- Nightshade vegetables like tomatoes, eggplants, capsicums, and potatoes can increase

inflammation in the body, especially in individuals with existing inflammatory conditions like arthritis.

Lesson 7: Recommendations for pH Balance
- Aim for a diet containing 80% alkaline-forming foods and 20% acid-forming foods to maintain a pH balance around 6.5 in the cells.
- Eliminate or reduce cane sugar, alcohol, caffeine, tobacco, and ideally meat and dairy products from the diet while increasing the consumption of vegetables and other alkaline-forming foods.

Lesson 8: Lifestyle Habits for pH Balance
- Proper oxygen intake through breathing, good posture, and exercise is essential for alkalizing the body.
- Sunshine, in moderation, helps convert cholesterol to vitamin D, which inhibits cancer cell growth.
- Temperance involves avoiding harmful substances like alcohol, caffeine, refined sugar, tobacco, drugs, and chemicals to maintain pH balance.
- Adequate rest, especially early in the night, contributes to an alkaline body state.
- The timing and composition of meals can affect the body's pH balance.
- Water should be consumed between meals, and adequate salt intake is essential for maintaining an alkaline state.
- Sodium should be consumed in its natural form, such as in unrefined sea salts like Celtic and Himalayan salts, to maintain mineral balance and alkalinity.
- Mental health, characterized by a positive attitude, laughter, faith, and hope, plays a crucial role in maintaining an alkaline state and overall well-being.

Lesson 9: Exercise for pH Balance
- Exercise, especially aerobic activities, helps increase oxygen availability to cells, which contributes to alkalinity.
- Aerobic exercise activates the release of the human growth hormone (HGH), leading to various health benefits.
- A minimum of 20 minutes of aerobic exercise a day is recommended, with one hour being ideal for reversing certain health problems.

Lesson 10: The Power of Laughter and Positive Thinking
- Laughter and positive thinking release healing hormones and contribute to an alkaline mental state.
- Negative emotions like fear, anxiety, and resentment can lead to physical health issues, while positive emotions like faith, hope, and trust promote healing and alkalinity.

Lesson 11: The Mind-Body Connection
- The mind and body are interconnected, and maintaining both physical and mental health is crucial for achieving and maintaining an alkaline state.
- Rewiring the brain is possible through diligence and exposure to positive influences.

REFLECTION QUESTIONS

Are you aware of the pH balance in your body and how it can impact your health? Reflect on your current diet and lifestyle choices and consider whether they are contributing to an acidic or alkaline internal environment.

What dietary changes can you make to shift towards a more alkaline-forming diet? Take a closer look at your food choices and explore ways to incorporate more alkaline-forming foods like fruits and vegetables while reducing acidic-forming ones.

How do your lifestyle habits, such as exercise, rest, and mental health practices, align with the goal of achieving an alkaline body state? Evaluate your daily routines and habits to determine whether they are helping or hindering your efforts to maintain pH balance.

Have you experienced the connection between your mental state and your physical health? Reflect on times when your emotional well-being influenced your physical health, and consider how fostering positive emotions can contribute to an alkaline body state.

What steps can you take to ensure that you're maintaining both physical and mental health in your journey towards optimal well-being?
Think about practical strategies for achieving and maintaining a balanced and alkaline body, both physically and mentally.

MILESTONE GOALS

Achieve and Maintain pH Balance: Your first goal can be to understand the concept of pH balance and take practical steps to maintain it in your body. This might involve assessing your current diet and making adjustments to include more alkaline-forming foods, reducing acidic foods, and monitoring your body's pH regularly.

Implement a Holistic Health Approach: Another goal could be to adopt a holistic approach to health that encompasses not only your dietary choices but also your exercise routines, rest patterns, and mental well-being. This could involve setting a fitness routine, improving sleep hygiene, and incorporating stress-reduction practices into your daily life.

Explore the Impact of Emotions on Health: Consider exploring the connection between your emotional state and your physical health. Set a goal to cultivate positive emotions and minimize stress, understanding that this can contribute to a more alkaline body state. This might involve practicing mindfulness, meditation, or seeking emotional support when needed.

ACTIONABLE MOVEMENTS

1. Assess Your Diet:

- Start by evaluating your current diet. Make a list of the foods you commonly consume and categorize them as acidic or alkaline-forming.
- Begin incorporating more alkaline-forming foods into your meals, such as leafy greens, fruits, and vegetables.

- Reduce the consumption of highly acidic foods like processed sugars, refined grains, and excessive animal proteins.

2. Stay Hydrated:

- Ensure you're drinking enough water throughout the day to stay hydrated. Aim for at least 2-3 liters of pure water daily.
- Avoid drinking water with meals, as it can dilute stomach acid needed for digestion. Instead, hydrate between meals.

3. Exercise Regularly:

- Establish a consistent exercise routine that includes at least 30 minutes of aerobic activity each day.
- Consider activities like walking, swimming, or gardening, which engage multiple muscle groups and promote overall well-being.

4. Prioritize Rest and Sleep:

- Create a sleep-friendly environment by ensuring your bedroom is dark, quiet, and cool.
- Aim for 7-9 hours of quality sleep each night, as it's crucial for your body's repair and rejuvenation.

5. Manage Stress and Emotions:

- Practice stress-reduction techniques such as deep breathing exercises.
- Foster positive emotions by engaging in activities that bring joy and fulfillment to your life.

6. Monitor pH Levels:

- Invest in pH test strips to periodically measure your body's pH levels, particularly in your urine and saliva.
- Use these measurements as a guide to assess the impact of dietary and lifestyle changes on your pH balance.

7. Educate Yourself Continuously:

- Continue to educate yourself about pH balance and holistic health by reading books, articles, and reputable sources on the topic.
- Stay informed about the latest research and insights related to maintaining a balanced body pH.

Record your reflections, insights, and observations on the concepts discussed earlier.

Use this space to brainstorm, sketch, or jot down any questions that arise in your mind. Make it a truly personal experience.

CHAPTER 11:
THE STOMACH'S SECRET WEAPON
HYDROCHLORIC ACID AND DIGESTION

Summary

"Sweet to the mouth, bitter to the stomach; bitter to the mouth, sweet to the stomach."
—*Anonymous*

In this chapter, the focus is on the essential role of Hydrochloric acid (HCl) in our body's self-healing mechanisms. HCl is a powerful enzyme produced in the liver and released into the stomach when we start consuming food. It plays a vital role in combating yeast and fungal issues in the body, acting as a potent fungicide. When HCl levels are optimal, a portion of it is absorbed into the bloodstream, where it acts as a guardian against blood-borne fungus.

Research suggests that as we age, starting from around 20 years old, most individuals experience a gradual decline in their digestive enzyme production, losing about 10 percent of these enzymes per decade. The chapter underscores the importance of maintaining adequate levels of HCl for proper digestion and overall health. In an ideal scenario, our food should be immersed in an HCl "pool" in the stomach, ideally ranging from 3200mg to 4000mg per meal.

Many people suffer from digestive issues like acid reflux and indigestion, primarily due to insufficient HCl production, leading to food lingering in the stomach without proper digestion. This undigested food can ferment, causing acidity and bloating. The liver is responsible for producing HCl, but it requires adequate hydration. Two cups of water per meal, consumed the day before, are necessary for the liver to produce the required HCl.

The chapter explains how HCl functions, including converting pepsinogen into pepsin, breaking down protein, and releasing essential nutrients from food. Additionally, HCl acts as a bactericide and fungicide, effectively eliminating harmful bacteria and fungi that may enter the body through food.

The role of gastrin, a gastrointestinal hormone, is discussed, as it stimulates the release of HCl and other digestive enzymes, promotes stomach wall cell growth, and increases gastric motility. Gastrin is released by G cells in response to various stimuli, such as the presence of different foods in the stomach, stomach distension, partially digested protein reaching the lower part of the stomach, and HCl contact with the stomach's mucosal lining.

The chapter provides practical tips to support HCl production and maintenance. These include drinking water between meals (avoiding water with meals to prevent HCl dilution), consuming lemon juice before or with meals to boost HCl activity, and incorporating protein into the initial mouthfuls of each meal to stimulate gastrin release. It emphasizes the importance of chewing food thoroughly, allowing for better enzyme action.

Furthermore, the chapter advises on the timing of meals and breaks between them, stressing the importance of giving the stomach time to digest and recover. Stress and anxiety during meals are cautioned against, as they can inhibit gastrin release. The chapter also mentions the benefits of consuming bitter herbs and foods known to stimulate HCl release.

For those who need additional support, Betaine Hydrochloride, an enzyme extracted from beetroot, is suggested as a powerful tool to increase stomach HCl levels. In some cases, proteolytic enzymes, which are essential for protein digestion, may be necessary. The chapter mentions various sources of proteolytic enzymes, including papain from pawpaw and bromelain from pineapple.

In summary, this chapter underscores the crucial role of Hydrochloric acid in our digestive system and overall health, offering practical advice and solutions for maintaining optimal HCl levels to support efficient digestion and combat various health issues.

LESSONS AND KEY POINTS FROM THIS CHAPTER

1. Hydrochloric acid (HCl) is a vital digestive enzyme produced in the liver and released into the stomach during digestion. It plays a crucial role in maintaining digestive health and combating fungal and bacterial issues in the body.

2. HCl levels decline with age, with research indicating that after the age of 20, most people experience a gradual decline in their digestive enzyme production, emphasizing the importance of maintaining optimal HCl levels for efficient digestion.

3. Inadequate HCl levels can lead to digestive problems, including common issues like acid reflux and indigestion. Low HCl levels result in undigested food fermenting in the stomach, causing acidity and bloating.

4. Hydration is essential for HCl production as the liver requires adequate hydration to produce HCl. Drinking two cups of water per meal the day before can help ensure sufficient HCl production.

5. HCl performs several crucial functions, including converting pepsinogen to pepsin (a proteolytic enzyme), breaking down proteins, releasing nutrients from food, and acting as a bactericide and fungicide.

6. Gastrin, a gastrointestinal hormone, plays a pivotal role as it stimulates the release of HCl and other digestive enzymes, promotes cell growth in the stomach wall, and increases gastric motility. Gastrin is triggered by various stimuli, including food in the stomach, stomach distension, partially digested protein, and HCl contact with the stomach lining.

7. Practical tips for HCl support include drinking water between meals (but avoiding it during meals), consuming lemon juice before or with meals, incorporating protein early in meals, and thoroughly chewing food.

8. Proper meal timing and allowing breaks between meals (approximately five hours) are essential for effective digestion and enzyme recovery. Avoiding unwanted stimulation between meals, such as eating snacks and chewing gum, is recommended.

9. Certain bitter herbs and foods like cayenne pepper, garlic, and ginger can stimulate HCl release and support digestion.

10. Supplements like Betaine Hydrochloride can help boost stomach acid levels in cases of HCl deficiency. Additionally, proteolytic enzymes from natural sources like papain and bromelain aid in protein digestion.

REFLECTION QUESTIONS

How conscious are you about your digestive health and the role of Hydrochloric acid (HCl) in it?

Have you ever experienced digestive issues such as acid reflux or indigestion? How do you think your HCl levels may have contributed to these problems?

What dietary habits do you currently have that may affect your HCl production and overall digestive health?

Are you aware of the impact of hydration on your body's ability to produce HCl? How can you ensure you stay adequately hydrated for optimal digestive function?

Have you ever considered incorporating bitter herbs or foods like cayenne pepper or ginger into your diet to support better digestion? How might you do so?

MILESTONE GOALS

Optimize Digestive Health: Your first goal could be to focus on optimizing your digestive health by paying more attention to your HCl levels and overall digestion. This might involve implementing practical tips mentioned in the chapter, such as drinking water between meals (and not during meals), consuming lemon juice before or with meals, and incorporating protein early in your meals. Your aim is to enhance your digestive processes and alleviate any discomfort caused by indigestion or acid reflux.

Hydration Consciousness: Given the importance of hydration for HCl production, your second goal could revolve around maintaining proper hydration habits. You can set a goal to drink two cups of water the day before each meal to support optimal HCl production. Ensuring you're well-hydrated when you sit down to eat can contribute to improved digestive function and overall well-being.

Incorporate Digestive-Boosting Foods: To further enhance your digestive health, you might aim to incorporate bitter herbs and foods that stimulate HCl release into your diet. Explore options such as cayenne pepper, garlic, ginger, or other mentioned herbs. Experiment with recipes or meal plans that include these ingredients to naturally support your body's digestive processes.

ACTIONABLE MOVEMENTS

1. Create a Hydration Schedule: Set a daily hydration goal that aligns with the recommendation in the chapter. Make it a habit to drink two cups of water the day before each meal to support HCl production. You can use a reusable water bottle to keep track of your daily intake.

2. Revise Your Meal Habits: Adjust your mealtime routines to optimize digestion. Stop drinking water 30 minutes before meals and resume drinking two hours later. This ensures that you don't dilute your stomach acid during meals, allowing for more effective digestion.

3. Include Digestive-Boosting Foods: Begin incorporating bitter herbs and foods known to stimulate HCl release into your meals. Experiment with recipes that include ingredients like cayenne pepper, garlic, ginger, or others mentioned in the chapter. You can gradually introduce these foods into your diet to enhance your digestion naturally.

4. Practice Mindful Eating: Focus on chewing your food slowly and thoroughly during meals. This helps break down food into smaller particles, making it easier for digestive enzymes to work effectively. Mindful eating also encourages you to be aware of the types of foods you consume and how they affect your digestion.

5. Monitor Digestive Health: Pay attention to any digestive issues you may experience, such as acid reflux or indigestion. Keep a journal to track when these issues occur and whether they correlate with your meal habits. This can help you pinpoint areas for improvement in your digestive health.

By taking these actionable movements, you can proactively work toward better digestive health and overall well-being, applying the knowledge and recommendations from the chapter.

Record your reflections, insights, and observations on the concepts discussed earlier.

Use this space to brainstorm, sketch, or jot down any questions that arise in your mind. Make it a truly personal experience.

CHAPTER 12:
LIVER
THE PROJECT MANAGER

Summary

The liver plays a pivotal role in maintaining overall health and combatting diseases. It serves as the body's project manager and master chemist, overseeing vital functions. It's crucial to ensure the liver functions optimally to support well-being. The liver is a remarkably busy organ, evident in its substantial blood flow. Approximately every 14 minutes, all of your blood circulates through this vital organ. Everything you ingest, whether it's food or toxins, first passes through the liver.

The liver's unique ability to heal itself and regenerate cells, particularly when supported nutritionally, sets it apart from other organs in the body. As the body's project manager, the liver decides how to handle each substance that enters it. When the liver operates efficiently, it helps prevent the development of diseases like cancer.

To better understand how to support the liver, it's essential to grasp its functions and the nutrients it requires:

1. Bile Salt Production: The liver manufactures bile salts, stored in the gall bladder and released in the small intestine to aid in fat emulsification and absorption.

2. Plasma Protein Production: Together with mast cells, the liver produces essential plasma proteins, including heparin, prothrombin, fibrinogen, and albumin.

3. Storage: The liver stores glycogen, copper, iron, and vitamins A, D, E, and K. It also stores certain toxins that can't be immediately broken down and expelled.

4. Nutrient Processing: The liver processes nutrients from the gastrointestinal tract, converting them into absorbable glucose, which is then used for energy, stored as glycogen, or converted into fat.

5. Hormone Regulation: The liver plays a crucial role in detoxifying excess estrogen, choosing between the 2-hydroxy and 16-hydroxy pathways, with implications for toxicity.

6. Detoxification: The liver detoxifies toxic substances, especially fat-soluble ones, through a three-phase process. In phase one, toxins are broken down into metabolites, which can sometimes become more toxic. Antioxidants, B vitamins, minerals, herbs, and fatty acids are necessary for this phase. Phase two conjugates metabolites with amino acids, making them water-soluble and safe for excretion. Sulphur-bearing amino acids, certain vegetables, and phytonutrients are crucial here. Phase three eliminates water-soluble toxins and requires essential fatty acids.

Maintaining a balance between these phases is essential for effective liver detoxification. A diet rich in legumes, grains, nuts, and seeds can provide essential amino acids required by the liver.

During fasting or detox programs, protein restriction can lead to diminished phase two activity, resulting in toxic metabolite accumulation and unpleasant symptoms. A liver cleanse lasting a week can help kickstart liver health, and for individuals with more severe health issues, this cleanse may need to be repeated over several months.

The liver's multifaceted functions and its remarkable ability to heal and detoxify the body underscore its critical role in maintaining well-being and combating diseases. Supporting the liver with the right nutrients and understanding its functions are crucial steps toward achieving optimal health.

Liver Cleanse

- 1 cup fresh orange and lemon juice
- 1 cup of pure water
- 1 clove of garlic*
- 1 tablespoon of olive oil*
- ½ a teaspoon of chopped ginger (this will negate any nausea).

1. Blend all ingredients
2. Drink upon rising on an empty stomach.

*As the week progresses, increase the garlic to four large cloves, and the olive oil to four tablespoons. Slowly increase as the body allows.

Fifteen minutes after this, cleanse your system by drinking two glasses of hot liver tea.

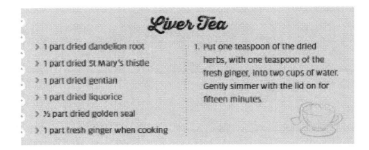

Liver Tea

> 1 part dried dandelion root
> 1 part dried St Mary's thistle
> 1 part dried gentian
> 1 part dried liquorice
> ½ part dried golden seal
> 1 part fresh ginger when cooking

1. Put one teaspoon of the dried herbs, with one teaspoon of the fresh ginger, into two cups of water. Gently simmer with the lid on for fifteen minutes.

During the week of this program, it's essential to cleanse the bowels daily by consuming about one cup of Colon Tea each night, adjusting the quantity based on individual colon health and needs. The goal is to achieve at least two bowel movements per day.

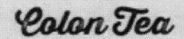

Colon Tea

> 1 part cascara segrada*
> 2 parts liquorice
> 3 parts buckthorn

1. Take one teaspoon of this tea mix to one cup of water. Gently simmer for fifteen minutes with the lid on.

* Cascara sagrada is a natural herbal laxative made from the reddish-brown bark of a tree (Rhamnus purshiana). It contains compounds called anthroquinones, which trigger contractions in the colon, causing the urge to have a bowel movement. Cascara sagrada can be found in various forms such as capsules, liquid extracts, and dried bark, which, when made into tea, can taste very bitter.

Castor oil is effective in penetrating deeply and can help break down lumps, bumps, and adhesions in the body. When used as part of a program, it can also soften and break down gallstones and lubricate the bile duct, making it easier for gravel or stones to be expelled. To benefit from this, it's recommended to wear a castor oil compress around the liver area for at least five hours daily, ideally in the week leading up to and during a liver cleanse.

LESSONS AND KEY POINTS FROM THIS CHAPTER

1. **The Liver's Vital Functions:** The liver is a crucial organ that serves as the body's project manager and master chemist. It oversees and regulates numerous vital functions in the body.

2. **Blood Circulation:** The liver has a significant blood flow, with all of your blood circulating through it approximately every 14 minutes. This emphasizes its importance in processing substances entering the body, including nutrients and toxins.

3. **Self-Healing and Regeneration:** The liver has a unique ability to heal itself and regenerate cells, especially when supported nutritionally. This capacity sets it apart from many other organs and contributes to overall health.

4. **Disease Prevention:** An efficiently operating liver can help prevent the development of diseases like cancer. Therefore, it's crucial to support the liver's optimal functioning.

5. **Key Liver Functions:** The chapter outlines several key functions of the liver, including bile salt production, plasma protein production, storage of essential nutrients and toxins, nutrient processing, hormone regulation, and detoxification.

6. **Detoxification Process:** Liver detoxification involves a three-phase process, where toxins are broken down into metabolites, conjugated with amino acids, and eliminated from the body. Various nutrients, amino acids, vegetables, and fatty acids are required for these phases.

7. **Balancing Detox Phases:** Maintaining a balance between the detoxification phases is essential for effective liver detoxification. A diet rich in legumes, grains, nuts, and seeds can provide essential amino acids required by the liver.

8. **Protein and Liver Health:** Protein restriction during fasting or detox programs can diminish phase two detoxification activity, leading to toxic metabolite accumulation and unpleasant symptoms. A week-long liver cleanse can help kickstart liver health.

9. **Repeat Cleanses:** For individuals with more severe health issues, repeated liver cleanses over several months may be necessary to support liver function effectively.

10. **Daily Bowel Cleansing:** During the cleanse program, it's crucial to cleanse the bowels daily using Colon Tea to ensure regular bowel movements.

11. **Castor Oil for Liver Health:** Castor oil can penetrate deeply into the body and help break down adhesions, including gallstones. Wearing a castor oil compress around the liver area for at least five hours daily during the cleanse can be beneficial.

12. **Liver Tea:** After the cleanse, it's recommended to drink two glasses of hot liver tea to further support liver health.

REFLECTION QUESTIONS

How conscious are you of the substances you consume and their potential impact on your liver's health?

Have you ever considered the importance of a well-functioning liver in disease prevention, and how do you prioritize its health in your lifestyle choices?

Do you incorporate foods rich in nutrients necessary for liver function into your daily diet?

Are you aware of any signs or symptoms that might indicate your liver's health needs attention, and if so, how do you plan to address them?

Have you ever explored or considered liver cleansing or detoxification practices as a means to support your overall well-being, and if not, what factors influence your decision in this regard?

MILESTONE GOALS

Enhance Liver Health Awareness: Your first goal can be to gain a deep understanding of the liver's vital functions and its pivotal role in maintaining overall health. This includes comprehending how it processes nutrients, detoxifies the body, and prevents diseases like cancer. By achieving this goal, you'll become more aware of the significance of liver health in your life.

Incorporate Liver-Friendly Practices: Set a goal to incorporate liver-friendly practices into your daily life. This may involve adjusting your diet to include foods that support liver function, avoiding substances harmful to the liver, and exploring detoxification or cleansing methods to kickstart liver health. By doing so, you aim to actively promote and maintain the well-being of this essential organ.

Implement a Liver Cleanse: Consider a specific goal of implementing a liver cleanse as outlined in the chapter, either as a one-week cleanse or as part of a more extended program. This goal can help you experience firsthand the benefits of supporting your liver's detoxification processes and improving its overall function.

ACTIONABLE MOVEMENTS

1. Replace Sugary Drinks: Take immediate action to eliminate sugary beverages from your diet, such as soda and excessive fruit juices. Replace them with water, herbal teas, or infused water with lemon or cucumber to reduce the sugar intake that can strain your liver.

2. Create a Liver-Friendly Meal Plan: Develop a specific meal plan that includes liver-supporting foods. For example, plan a week of meals rich in vegetables, lean proteins, and whole grains, while minimizing processed foods and saturated fats.

3. Daily Exercise Routine: Start a daily exercise routine that includes at least 30 minutes of physical activity, such as brisk walking, jogging, or cycling. Regular exercise can improve liver function and overall health.

4. Set Up a Detoxification Schedule: Establish a schedule for liver detoxification practices, such as a one-week liver cleanse as mentioned in the chapter. Mark your calendar and gather the necessary supplies to initiate the process.

Record your reflections, insights, and observations on the concepts discussed earlier.

Use this space to brainstorm, sketch, or jot down any questions that arise in your mind. Make it a truly personal experience.

CHAPTER 13: RECIPES

Dear reader,

We understand that you're eager to explore some delicious recipes, but unfortunately, we cannot provide full recipe details in this summary. To fully benefit from these mouthwatering creations, we encourage you to visit the original source "Self Heal by Design by Barbara O'Neil" to find this chapter where these recipes are featured. There, you'll find all the intricate details, ingredients, and instructions needed to recreate these culinary delights to perfection.

Happy cooking and bon appétit!

EPILOGUE

As we reach the end of the workbook, we embark on a profound journey of self-discovery and transformation. Throughout this workbook, we shared Barbara's wisdom, insights, and practical guidance on harnessing the incredible power of micro-organisms to optimize our health.

We've learned about the intricate ecosystems within our bodies, the microbiome, and the pivotal role it plays in our physical and mental well-being. Barbara's words have illuminated the path to understanding how our lifestyle choices, nutrition, and environment impact these micro-organisms and, in turn, our overall health.

As we close this chapter, let us remember that self-healing is a continuous process, and this workbook is merely the beginning. The knowledge and tools you've acquired here are the foundation upon which you can build a healthier and more harmonious life. Barbara's teachings remind us that we have the power to nurture our microbiome, support our immune system, and cultivate vitality from within.

Take these lessons to heart, and may they serve as a constant reminder that self-healing is a journey of empowerment and self-love. Continue to explore, experiment, and adapt the principles outlined in this workbook to suit your unique needs. Remember that health is not an endpoint but a lifelong endeavor.

In closing, we express our gratitude to Barbara O'Neill for sharing her expertise and passion for natural health with us. Let us move forward with the knowledge that we can design our own path to wellness and embrace the innate capacity of our bodies to heal.

Wishing you a vibrant and fulfilling life filled with health, happiness, and self-discovery.

ABOUT US.

Jen Press is a group of avid readers who were passionate about learning and self-improvement. They loved to read books and attend seminars, but they often found themselves overwhelmed by the sheer volume of information available. They struggled to remember everything they had learned and to apply it to their daily lives.

One day, they decided to create a solution to their problem: an association that would provide the best summary books and workbooks on the market. They believed that by distilling the key concepts and takeaways from the most impactful books and seminars, they could help others learn and grow in a more efficient and effective way.

They worked tirelessly to curate the most valuable content and distill it into easy-to-digest summaries and workbooks. They tested and refined their methods until they had perfected their approach, creating an association that was known for its quality and reliability.

Their mission was to empower people to learn and improve themselves, no matter how busy their lives might be. They wanted to make it easy and accessible for anyone to access the insights and knowledge that could transform their lives.

As the association grew, it became a trusted resource for readers and learners around the world. It helped people to discover new ideas, gain new perspectives, and develop new skills. And most importantly, it helped them to take action and make positive changes in their lives.

Today, this brand is known as the leading provider of summary books and workbooks on the market. Its products have helped countless individuals to learn, grow, and achieve their goals. Its story is a testament to the power of learning and the potential of every individual to improve themselves and their lives.

We welcome any suggestions or feedback that can help us improve our books. If you have any advice or recommendations, please feel free to contact us via email. We value your input and look forward to hearing from you.

jenpress.workbooks@gmail.com

Thank you!

We are constantly striving to provide the ideal experience for the community, and your input helps us to define that experience. So we kindly ask you when you have free time take a minute to post a review on Amazon.

Thank you for helping us support our passions.

TO LEAVE A REVIEW, JUST SCAN THE QR CODE BELOW:

OR YOU CAN GO TO:

amazon.com/review/create-review/

Made in the USA
Las Vegas, NV
28 October 2023

79837517R00072